The Politics
of Normalcy

THE NORTON ESSAYS IN AMERICAN HISTORY

Under the general editorship of
HAROLD M. HYMAN
William P. Hobby Professor of American History
Rice University

EISENHOWER AND BERLIN, 1945: THE DECISION
TO HALT AT THE ELBE   *Stephen E. Ambrose*

THE MONEY QUESTION DURING RECONCTRUCTION
                             Walter T. K. Nugent

ANDREW JACKSON AND THE BANK WAR
                             Robert V. Remini

THE GREAT BULL MARKET: WALL STREET IN THE 1920's
                             Robert Sobel

THE JACKSONIAN ECONOMY   *Peter Temin*

A NEW ENGLAND TOWN: THE FIRST HUNDRED YEARS
                             Kenneth A. Lockridge

DIPLOMACY FOR VICTORY: FDR AND UNCONDITIONAL
SURRENDER   *Raymond G. O'Connor*

THE ORIGINS OF AMERICAN INTERVENTION IN THE
FIRST WORLD WAR   *Ross Gregory*

THE POLITICS OF NORMALCY: GOVERNMENTAL THEORY
AND PRACTICE IN THE HARDING-COOLIDGE ERA
                             Robert Murray

THE IMPEACHMENT AND TRIAL OF ANDREW JOHNSON
                             Michael Les Benedict

THE GENET MISSION   *Harry Ammon*

The Politics
of Normalcy

*Governmental Theory and Practice
in the Harding-Coolidge Era*

Robert K. Murray

New York W · W · NORTON & COMPANY · INC ·

Library of Congress Cataloging in Publication Data

Murray, Robert K
    The politics of normalcy.

    Bibliography: p.
    1. Harding, Warren Gamaliel, Pres. U.S., 1865–
1923. 2. Coolidge, Calvin, Pres. U.S., 1872–1933.
3. United States—Politics and government—1921–1923.
I. Title

E786.M83   973.91'4'0924   72–8354

ISBN 0–393–05474–8

ISBN 0–393–09422–7 (pbk.)

        1 2 3 4 5 6 7 8 9 0

For Sarah, Rudy, and Russell
who knew the joys and sorrows of life
and by their loving example
showed a growing boy
how to accept
both

Contents

Foreword

THE POLITICAL aspects of the 1920s have long been a subject of contempt and derision for most observers of the American scene. Historical writers from Samuel Hopkins Adams to Samuel Eliot Morison have portrayed the political developments of the decade in an extremely unflattering manner and have usually singled out the early years of the period for special condemnation. The Harding administration, in particular, has borne the brunt of these assaults and has traditionally been cited to prove that the era was devoid of political accomplishment, barren of public benefit, and riddled with government scandals.

Renewed historical interest in the 1920s has prompted a reexamination of this traditional position. The older antagonistic writings of such progressive journalists as William Allen White and Frederick Lewis Allen have come under careful scrutiny, while the loose interpretations of some modern liberal historians, like Arthur M. Schlesinger, Jr., have been similarly challenged. The increasing availability of autobiographical and manuscript materials for the Roaring Twenties has provided contemporary students with a host of new insights and has encouraged an altered view of the decade.

I was fortunate to be among the first scholars to gain access to the Harding Papers when they were released to the public in Columbus, Ohio, in 1964. Moreover, I was one of the few who braved the cold of the Iowa hinterland when the Hoover Presidential Library opened its treasures not long thereafter. Both the Harding and Hoover collections proved to be rich mines of

new information on the 1920s. Through them I became particularly interested in the Harding story, especially the Greek-
like tragedy of Warren Harding himself. But I was also intrigued
by the exaggerations, the distortions, the misinformation, and
the myths that had gathered around the early 1920s as a whole.

In 1969 the first results of my investigation were published
in a lengthy book entitled *The Harding Era: Warren G. Harding
and His Administration.* The nature of that enterprise afforded
me the opportunity to explore the realities and explode some
of the myths of Harding's specific situation. While that effort
will not be repeated here, it is only fair to state that I still hold
the same general views about Harding as a politician and about
the Harding administration as a formative historical force that
I held three years ago. Since then, however, I have had time to
reflect more deeply both on the Harding period and on the
years that immediately followed. Moreover, I have since been
exposed to important new collections of contemporary manuscript materials—the Alfred E. Smith Papers, the John W.
Davis Papers, the Thomas J. Walsh Papers, the William G.
McAdoo Papers, and the Robert M. LaFollette Papers. Such
reflection and exposure have caused me to see the Harding-
Coolidge succession as a complementary political unit and have
given me a fuller appreciation of the complexities involved in
the creation of what has traditionally been viewed as the relatively unsophisticated political program known as "normalcy."

Three years ago I was so anxious to revise old myths and
set the record straight about Harding that I concentrated heavily
on documentation and the authentication of facts. I wanted to
establish precisely the details of Harding's presidential career
and pinpoint the various activities of his administration. In
addition, I wanted to ascertain the relative success or failure
of his administration's policies in the areas of farm legislation,
labor, business, foreign affairs, race relations, prohibition enforcement, and so on. The result was primarily analytical and
descriptive.

This present volume is intended to be more interpretive and
freewheeling. Specifically, I will attempt to show more clearly

the reasons for the lure of the Republicans in 1920 and evaluate more fully the catalytic role played by Harding. I will
explore the political philosophy underlying "normalcy," the
administrative means whereby that program was instituted, the
uniqueness of Harding's "best minds" executive system, and
the various conflicting views concerning the proper roles of the
president and Congress. I will examine congressional attitudes,
the nature of the divisions in Congress, and the development of
executive-legislative hostility during the period. I will analyze
the gap between the theory and the practice of normalcy in
the years before 1925, the gradual shift in White House thinking on presidential functions, the struggle involved in the attempt to have government operate "without excess," the
significance of Coolidge's election, and the final coalescence
of normalcy theory and practice. Finally, I will review the impact of the scandals and their accompanying rhetoric on political developments during 1923–25 in the hope of conveying to
the reader that political morality and immorality are only relative terms, that neither is the exclusive possession of any person
or any party, and that even the loftiest ideals and the most
sincere eloquence are sometimes infected with the basest of
political motives.

In the preparation of this study, I was aided by the Central
Fund for Research of the Pennsylvania State University and by
the Office of Research of the Liberal Arts College, which provided financial support when it was needed. I also owe a debt
to the enlightened research-leave policy of the Department of
History, which supplied something money cannot buy—time.
To Harold Hyman, the general editor of the Norton Essays in
American History, goes my gratitude for inviting me to participate in this series and for shepherding this project through
the editorial maze. To my colleagues in the Penn State History
Department, who have had to suffer through endless lunch-
time discourses on Wilson, Harding, and Coolidge, I offer both
my thanks and my condolences. Again, as in the past, my wife,
Eve, has had to bear the major burden during the birth of this
manuscript. I now apologize for those second and third calls

to dinner, the uncleaned basement, the unraked leaves, and the unmowed lawn. Doctoring an ailing sentence and administering to a poorly organized paragraph has a way of causing me to hear yet not hear, see but not see, and forget even the most elemental family responsibilities.

As for the three named on the dedication page, the remaining one knows what I mean.

ROBERT K. MURRAY

State College, Pennsylvania
April 15, 1972

The Politics
of Normalcy

ABBREVIATIONS

The following abbreviations have been used in the footnotes.

AHR   *American Historical Review*

HHP   Herbert C. Hoover Papers

HMD   Harry M. Daugherty

HP   Warren G. Harding Papers

JAH   *Journal of American History*

LC   Library of Congress, Washington, D.C.

MVHR *Mississippi Valley Historical Review*

OHRO Oral History Research Office, Columbia University

OHSL Ohio Historical Society Library, Columbus, Ohio

NICB National Industrial Conference Board

NYPL New York Public Library

WGH Warren G. Harding

1

The Great Mandate
of 1920

~~~~~~

ON THE EVE of the presidential election of 1920, an excited
Florence Harding wrote to a friend: "We are going to win, and
win BIG." [1] The next day, while her husband and his campaign
manager, Harry M. Daugherty, played a leisurely round of
golf, millions of voters trooped to the polls and made Florence
Harding's prophecy come true.

It was a fantastic victory. Newspaper headlines groped for
superlatives, while politicians were stunned. George Sutherland,
one of Harding's campaign workers, said it was "the most joyous
thing that ever happened." Joseph P. Tumulty, President Wilson's private secretary, moaned: "It was a landslide, it was an
earthquake." Franklin Roosevelt, the defeated Democratic candidate for vice-president, wrote at the head of a letter to a
friend: "Franklin D. Roosevelt, Ex V.P., Canned. (Errone-
ously reported dead)." [2]

The vote, as recorded by the New York *Times,* was 16,181,-
289 for Harding; 9,141,750 for James M. Cox; and 941,827
for Eugene V. Debs (Socialist). Harding carried thirty-seven of
the forty-eight states and received 404 electoral votes. His popular majority (60.2 percent) was the largest yet recorded in the

1. Mrs. Harding to a friend, October 25, 1920, HP (OHSL), Box
353, folder 2521–1, item 146749.
2. Frank Freidel, *Franklin D. Roosevelt: The Ordeal* (Boston,
1954), 91; Joel F. Paschal, *Mr. Justice Sutherland: A Man Against the
State* (Princeton, 1951), 107.

nation's history. As a result of the election, the Republican party controlled the House 303 to 131, the widest margin in the party's annals. In the Senate, the Republicans not only retained all their own seats but captured ten from the Democrats, giving them a majority of twenty-four.

With this stunning Republican victory, the so-called Age of Normalcy began, spanning the years of the 1920s and offering to the American people a conservative approach to national problems and politics. "Normalcy" was regarded as an anachronism by many later observers, who found more to admire in the preceding Progressive Era and in the subsequent New Deal. But Harding's triumph was not a fluke. It did not reveal a lapse in national common sense, nor did it indicate a degeneration of the country's moral fiber. As a political system, "normalcy" embraced traditionally understandable and historically acceptable methods for dealing with the nation's ills and fitted neatly into the American post–World War I milieu.

Over the years, a number of reasons have been given for the Republicans' remarkable showing in 1920, some of questionable value. It has been claimed that there was a poor voter turnout in 1920 (only 49.3 percent of those eligible voted) and that therefore the Republican endorsement was more negative than positive. It has also been charged that the Republicans "bought" the election with large expenditures of money. Some observers later said that the League of Nations issue was the downfall of the Democrats, or that "the times" foreordained that a Harding-type politician would be elected to the White House. Still others claimed that the chief reason for the change was a public reaction against the policies of Wilson.[3]

None of these arguments really explain the tremendous lure of the Republicans in 1920 or the emergence of public sentiment favoring "normalcy." Only the last—the reaction against Wilsonism—begins to strike at the heart of the matter. Indeed,

3. For an analysis of these factors, see Robert K. Murray, *The Harding Era: Warren G. Harding and His Administration* (Minneapolis, 1969), 66–69, 71–91.

by 1920 the public had grown weary of Wilson and all his trappings. In particular, the twenty-four months between the armistice and election day had been plagued by extreme confusion and turmoil. As one postwar problem succeeded another, the nation found itself confronted by a set of circumstances for which it was totally unprepared and which it only partially understood.

First, there was the problem of demobilization and the liquidation of mountains of military supplies and property. Rather than face up boldly to this problem, the Wilson administration merely muddled through, ignoring the resultant waste and inefficiency. In the meantime, state and local authorities, businesses, unions, and farm organizations rushed forward to implement their own postwar schemes. Simultaneously, the sudden termination of war contracts amounting to $35 billion dealt a staggering blow to the industrial community, and the wartime employment figure of 40 million skidded sharply. By February 1919 an estimated 3 million persons were unemployed, and this condition continued into the summer.[4]

After June 1919 an upsurge in the economy caused a decline in unemployment, but it was accompanied by a ruinous rise in prices. The effect on the average citizen's pocketbook was disastrous. By November 1919 the cost of living was 82.2 percent above the 1914 level. By July 1920 it stood at 104.5 percent, the biggest jumps being in clothing and food. Since wages and salaries did not keep pace with this runaway inflation, grumbling was heard everywhere. Union men walked picket lines, housewives went on buying strikes, and congressmen loudly debated legislation for economic controls, while calling on President Wilson and his administration to do something. The press in particular condemned Wilson for worrying about the salvation of the world (i.e., the League of Nations) at a time

4. On demobilization see Paul A. Samuelson and Everett E. Hagen, *After the War, 1918–1920: Military and Economic Demobilization of the United States* (n.p., 1943); and James R. Mock and Evangeline Thurber, *Report on Demobilization* (Norman, Okla., 1944).

when the high cost of living was "killing" the people of the United States.[5]

During the worst of this inflation, President Wilson lay desperately ill in the White House.[6] From late September 1919, when he suffered his first stroke, until the end of his term in March 1921, the nation remained virtually leaderless, while grave political and social disruptions, along with rampant inflation, ravaged the country. Specifically, the struggle in the Senate over the League added to the general confusion. So did rising public fears of a radical revolution. A few domestic radical stirrings, inspired by the success of the Bolsheviki in Russia, served as the factual basis for this scare. But government officials, the press, and common citizens alike rapidly succumbed to a form of mass neurosis that condoned the violent repression of even the most innocuous "unpatriotic" activity. Before the "Red scare" abated, normally rational citizens helped tar and feather suspected radicals, mounted surveillance on ministers and schoolteachers, passed loyalty-oath legislation, and applauded as immigrant ("Red") meeting places were raided by government officials and suspected subversives were deported to Russia.[7]

The worst aspects of this hysteria passed by the late spring of 1920, but not before the inflation-riddled economy again collapsed. The first sign was a break in agricultural prices in May. Then other wholesale prices began to fall, sometimes at a rate of 3 percent a month. The cost of living dropped from 104.5 percent above the 1914 level in July 1920 to 93.1 percent in March 1921—the sharpest slide for any comparable period in American history.[8]

5. Statistics are from reports of the NICB. For example, see NICB, *Changes in the Cost of Living, July, 1914–March, 1922* (Report No. 49, New York, 1922), 31, 33.

6. Best on Wilson's illness is Gene Smith, *When the Cheering Stopped: The Last Years of Woodrow Wilson* (New York, 1964).

7. For the "Red scare," see Robert K. Murray, *Red Scare: A Study in National Hysteria, 1919–1920* (Minneapolis, 1955).

8. See NICB, *Changes in the Cost of Living, July, 1914–March, 1922,* 31, 33.

The effect of this sudden deflation was staggering, Hardest hit was the farmer. Between July and December 1920, the average price of the ten leading crops fell 57 percent; by May 1921, these prices were only one-third what they had been in June 1920. Farm income fell commensurately. By the winter of 1921, farm incomes were 50 percent below their 1919 levels. At the same time, farm bankruptcies sharply increased while land values declined. Caught with overextended credit in machinery and farm land, many rural banks went under, further increasing farm distress.[9]

Although less disastrously affected, labor and industry also suffered from this deflation. In July 1920, labor's earnings began to fall and continued to do so throughout 1921. Mounting unemployment and a decrease in business activity inevitably followed. Having just recovered from the dislocations of the immediate postwar period, the labor market quickly became glutted. It was estimated that in January 1921 there were 3,-473,446 fewer persons in industrial employment than in January 1920. This represented an unemployment rate of almost 20 percent.[10]

Many of these factors were unquestionably in the minds of voters when they went to the polls in late 1920. The Wilson administration had apparently failed. Its legacy was a potpourri of unsolved problems and mounting frustrations. Business had suffered through a slipshod and haphazard reconversion period only to experience the wrench of a shaky boom followed by a tragic bust. Businessmen now demanded a new and more sympathetic approach to the nation's industrial problems. Likewise, labor, faced with over 3 million unemployed, desired quick government action to restore prosperity—and jobs. Farmers, evidencing signs of bitter rebellion, clamored for easier credit and other remedial farm legislation. All these elements—busi-

9. For the best coverage of the farm depression, see James H. Shideler, *Farm Crisis, 1919–1923* (Berkeley, 1957).
10. Statistics are from NICB, *The Unemployment Problem* (Report No. 43, New York, 1921), 9–10.

nessmen, workingmen, and farmers—helped swell Republican
totals on election day as they recoiled from the adverse effect of
what was collectively and derisively labeled "Wilsonism."

Still, the reasons for the Republican victory in 1920 remain
incomplete without consideration of the positive appeal of the
Republicans and especially of their candidate, Warren G. Harding. Harding was born on November 2, 1865, and grew up in
the gentle rolling Ohio countryside around the small town of
Marion.[11] Trying his hand first at schoolteaching and then at
selling insurance, he finally turned to journalism, and in 1884
bought the decrepit five-column, four-page Marion *Star* for
$300. As publisher, Harding rapidly nursed the *Star* into robust
health and by the turn of the century was one of Marion's leading citizens. Entering politics, between the years 1899 and 1915
he served two terms in the Ohio state senate and one term as
lieutenant governor. In 1914, his charming personality, his
reputation as a conciliator, and his services to the Taft faction
combined to win him election to the United States Senate, a
position he greatly enjoyed.

Harding passed the years 1915–19 unspectacularly. While
not the nonentity that some observers later called him, he was
unobtrusive on the Senate floor and certainly did not appear to
be presidential timber. As in the Ohio senate, he was successful
in making himself popular on both sides of the aisle. Among his
friends were not only many of the Republican leaders of the
Senate but such powerful Democratic senators as Oscar W.
Underwood and Gilbert M. Hitchcock. He and Mrs. Harding,
a plain-featured, sharp-tongued woman whom he had married
in 1891, were prominent in Washington society's "four hundred," and his home was a mecca for weekend entertaining and
for card playing with such Senate cronies as Albert B. Fall,
Frederick Hale, and Joseph S. Frelinghuysen.

In 1919, when the political atmosphere began to heat up
over the League of Nations issue, Harding again played a minor

11. For the most recent and complete account of Harding's early
life, emphasizing political developments, see Randolph C. Downes,
The Rise of Warren Gamaliel Harding, 1865–1920 (Columbus, 1970).

role. He opposed the League simply because he believed his Ohio constituents were against it. As a member of the powerful Foreign Relations Committee, he was privy to all discussions regarding the League and was one of the group that called on the White House in mid-August 1919 to air their differences with President Wilson. Still, he was never comfortable in the same voting bloc with "irreconcilables" like William E. Borah and Hiram Johnson, and he deplored the use of the "truth squads" the anti-League faction sent out to harass Wilson on his ill-fated western trip.

Harding's interest in the presidency was not originally kindled by his wife or by the Ohio politician Harry Daugherty, as is usually claimed, but by a small group of friends—Charles E. Hard, owner of the Portsmouth *Daily Blade;* George B. Christian, Jr., a Marion neighbor; F. E. Scobey, a former Ohioan living in Texas; and E. Mont Reily, a member of the Missouri Republican Committee and the originator of the phrase "Harding and Back to Normal." At first, Harding took the prodding of these men as mere flattery and turned it aside. But the death of Theodore Roosevelt in 1919, the bitterness of the League fight, and the fluid political situation in Ohio made him change his mind. Mainly, it was his fear that certain pro-Roosevelt elements (which contained considerable anti-Harding sentiment) might seize the Ohio party machinery and force his retirement from the Senate that ultimately drove him to take the plunge. To declare for the presidency seemed a sure way to maintain his influence in Ohio and guarantee his reelection to the Senate. As he wrote Scobey, "The only thing disagreeable about it is that I despise being forced into the position of being a presidential aspirant." [12]

Harry Daugherty, known primarily for his clever political manipulations and Ohio lobbying techniques, now stepped forward as the coordinator of all pro-Harding activities. Beginning in December 1919, Daugherty and Harding, working as a team, solicited support from all quarters but carefully refrained from

12. WGH to Scobey, November 22, 1919, HP, Box 759, folder 5, items 321130–32.

appearing too eager or aggressive.[13] Their success was such that by the time of the June convention, they decided to convert Harding's original plan for mere political survival in Ohio into a serious drive for national power. Still, they were careful to draw only modest attention to Harding's candidacy, antagonized no favorite sons, and quietly continued to pick up second- and third- choice support in many delegations. Just before the convention opened, Albert Fall confided to a worried Harding supporter, "They say Warren Harding is not getting newspaper publicity. Well, I'm glad he isn't. But you haven't heard anyone say that Warren Harding is making any enemies anywhere, have you? That's the answer. Harding will be nominated." [14]

Fall's words were prophetic. When the Chicago convention bogged down in a deadlock between the two front-runners, Governor Frank O. Lowden of Illinois and General Leonard Wood, the delegates finally turned to the Ohio senator. Allegedly, this resulted from machinations and deals consummated late one Friday night in a "smoke-filled room" in the Hotel Blackstone. No myth has been more pervasive in American history than this one, but it is just that—a myth. There was a Friday-night political conference held in a Blackstone suite rented by the Republican National Committee chairman, Will H. Hays. But no orders ever went to convention delegates as a result of it, nor did it signal the implementation of a senatorial plan to nominate Harding. Of the sixteen senators at the convention, thirteen continued to vote for candidates other than Harding on the first four ballots on Saturday morning. Even after the convention reconvened for the ninth ballot on Saturday afternoon and rumors were flying of an impending Harding victory, only three of the thirteen switched to the Ohioan, leaving ten still voting for other candidates. Far from supporting Harding, a few of

13. The basic source on Daugherty's activities is Harry M. Daugherty Papers (OHSL) as well as HP. Sample Harding letter is WGH to J. H. Rossiter, January 20, 1920, HP, Box 690, folder 4972–1, item 316124.
14. Kathleen Lawlor manuscript in HP, Box 797, folder 2, quoting Fall.

these senators, such as Henry Cabot Lodge, used the Saturday recess to attempt to create a stop-Harding movement.[15]

Contrary to myths concerning smoke-filled rooms, senate cabals, and the like, Harding's nomination was no mystery. The fact that it could come about so naturally, given the circumstances, prompted many to disbelieve its simplicity. From the time of the Lowden-Wood deadlock, Harding became the most available candidate. At that moment, Harding's rejection would have been more surprising than his nomination. The move toward his banner happened spontaneously. As Senator James W. Wadsworth of New York later explained, the motivation behind the Harding nomination was "psychological. . . . The delegates did it themselves!" [16]

Except for his famous "normalcy" speech, in which he declared to a Boston audience that "America's present need is not heroics but healing; not nostrums but normalcy," Harding's contributions to the campaign of 1920 have been largely ignored. Yet Harding was an important factor in the ensuing Republican victory. He set the tone of the campaign by trying to cool the superheated political atmosphere and soothe public fears. He showed that he would not be an obstinate leader of the Wilson type and that he desired only to marshal the energies of the government to help business, labor, and agriculture get back on their feet. Appearing humble and non-disputatious, Harding said the right things and appealed to the right instincts.

The success of this approach was first evident in Republican ranks. Badly splintered, the Republican party appeared initially to be too weak to mount a vigorous assault on its Democratic opponents. Yet, by election day, Harding succeeded in enticing

15. For a demolition of the smoke-filled room and Senate cabal myths, see Harry S. New, "The Senatorial Oligarchy," *Saturday Evening Post,* CCIV (May 28, 1932), 84, and Wesley M. Bagby, "The 'Smoke-Filled Room' and the Nomination of Warren G. Harding," *MVHR,* XLI, No. 4 (March 1955), 657–74.

16. "Reminiscences of James W. Wadsworth," OHRO, 275; James Wadsworth to Cyril Clemens, November 14, 1947, Cyril Clemens Papers (OHSL), Box 3.

all dissident groups back into the party fold. He miraculously received promises of support not only from regular Republicans and the Old Guard—men like Lodge, Boies Penrose, Frank B. Brandegee, and Philander C. Knox—but also from such diverse liberal and progressive elements as Robert M. LaFollette, Hiram Johnson, Fiorello LaGuardia, Charles Evans Hughes, Herbert Hoover, Frank Lowden, and even General Wood—men who would never again work for the same presidential candidate.

At the same time, the Republican cause greatly benefited from a smoothly operating campaign machine. Will Hays, who continued as chairman of the Republican National Committee, kept close watch over finances and party organization, while Harry Daugherty shrewdly supervised campaign strategy. Harding himself proved to be highly adaptable and a marked asset. He agreed with the decision to run a "front porch" campaign because it seemed "dignified." He also cooperated willingly with Albert D. Lasker, the famous Chicago advertising executive, who used him in all sorts of publicity stunts, including shaking hands with movie stars and posing with Al Jolson, who came all the way from New York to Marion to sing "Harding, You're the Man for Us." Such contrived publicity, as well as the front-porch, tactic, might have seemed overdone with another candidate. But not with Harding. His various activities were avidly followed by the general public because he was so likable and so readily believable. Harding never pretended to be other than he was—a mild, simple, average man, suddenly thrown into the spotlight of national attention and loving it. If Republican campaign strategy and publicity committed excesses in 1920, they were not of distortion but of making a virtue of the reality.

Within this setting the Republicans made an excellent showing, and their candidate was a superb campaigner. Harding avoided personalities, refused to attack the sick Wilson, and was never pretentious as his Democratic opponent, Governor Cox of Ohio, often was. Standing on his own front porch in Marion, greeting delegations in his white trousers, blue coat, and sawtooth straw hat, Harding was the picture of respectability. As one observer noted, while Cox "was campaigning all over the lot, in a sweat, in his mental shirt sleeves, with his coat off, ringing fire alarms," Harding appeared as "a quiet gentleman who had no beads on his forehead, no dust on his shoes, no red in his eye." [17] This contrast alone enhanced Harding's image, and undecided voters could not fail to be impressed.

In their desire to denigrate both the Harding image and the entire Republican performance after 1920, most historians have slighted the fact that America liked both what it saw and what it heard from the front porch. The views that Harding expressed were a carefully constructed composite of the best Republican thinking at the time and represented what was generally meant by "a return to normalcy." Some of these views were designed to attract the support of businessmen and were first worked over for the candidate by his chief business adviser, former Senator John W. Weeks. Some views were specifically tailored for the agricultural community, first being refined by Henry C. Wallace, Harding's agricultural adviser. Other positions were similarly delineated with the laborer, the consumer, and "Mr. Average Citizen" in mind. In any case, the Republican candidate's speeches intelligibly and accurately defined the conservative Republican position as of 1920, and to a nation growing weary of Wilsonian liberalism these utterances possessed considerable appeal.

Harding's front-porch remarks clearly presaged what he would do if elected president. He declared, for example, for an emergency tariff to protect domestic farm products until a new permanent tariff could be enacted. He also advocated the passage of other remedial legislation for the farmer, particularly an extension of rural credits. He voiced suspicion of foreign infiltration, especially by the "newer" immigrant, and suggested a tighter immigration policy. He wanted a big navy and an enlarged merchant marine. He paid lip service to trade-unionism and collective bargaining, but he bluntly opposed union dictation of any kind to either business or government. He promised

17. White to WGH, October 5, 1920, HP, Box 536, folder 4220–1, item 244703.

the elimination of excess-profits taxes and the lowering of sur-taxes on private incomes. He declared himself in favor of economy in government and of the creation of a national budget system for reducing and controlling federal expenditures. He promised to work for an anti-lynching law for Negroes. Most of all, he advocated allowing the nation to experience a period of tranquillity during which it could reestablish "normalcy" and resume its prosperous ways.[18]

The traditional notion that Harding and the Republicans were vapid and imprecise in the campaign of 1920 rests almost exclusively on their handling of the League of Nations problem. This was admittedly traumatic for them. From the time of Harding's acceptance speech in late July, he was badgered, tugged, and prodded by the various conflicting elements in his party. Senator Lodge believed this would be the major issue and pleaded with Harding to "bear down" on the question. Other opponents of the League, either "strict reservationists" or "ir-reconcilables," also bombarded Harding with appeals to "stand firm." There is no question that in the early days of the campaign the Republican candidate was more influenced by these men than by pro-Leaguers. But as time went by, Harding moved to a more neutral position and finally succeeded, through calculated and uncalculated ambiguity, in convincing Republican pro-Leaguers like Herbert Hoover and Charles Evans Hughes that his election was the surest way to bring the United States not into "the Wilson League" but into some kind of "an association of nations." [19]

Harding later told a friend: "It was impossible to harmo-nize my advisers on the subject of the League, and ultimately I took the course which seemed to me to be best." [20] One might fault the Republican candidate on his trimming, his lack of

18. Harding's front-porch speeches were reported in the press of the day, beginning on July 31 and continuing to September 25, 1920.
19. Lodge-Harding correspondence on the League is in HP, Box 544, folder 4270–1; for Hoover, see HHP (Hoover Presidential Library, West Branch, Iowa), Box AK 1–7 and Box 1–Q/89.
20. WGH to F. H. Gillett, August 30, 1920, HP, Box 543, folder 4267–1, item 247579.

specificity, and his conscious ambiguity. But his amazing success in keeping all these conflicting groups campaigning together was no mean tribute to his political talent. The Democrats, meanwhile, reveled in the apparent disorder in the Republican camp on the League issue. Cox, who supported the League, said all he had to do to gather ammunition for the day's campaigning was to read the morning newspapers and discover the latest contradiction in Republican attitudes. But Cox's sallies against the Republicans did not sway the public, and it somehow retained a greater interest in Harding's vague and misty views on "an association of nations" than in Cox's pro-League commitment.

In emphasizing the League problem and Republican confusion over it, Cox was obviously trying to capitalize on what he and his advisers thought was their strongest issue. In comparison with other possibilities, it probably was. But the Democrats really had no potent issue in 1920—a fact that Cox glumly perceived as the campaign progressed. Cox's attempts to revive voter enthusiasm by recalling the triumphant reforms of the prewar New Freedom failed dismally, and his laudatory acclaim for the Clayton Act, the Federal Reserve Act, and so on, met with indifference. His talk about expanding the usefulness of such reforms seemed irrelevant, while his infrequent admission that there were some defects in the last Wilson years gained him few votes. What currently mattered was the existence of unemployment, high taxes, business depression, farmer unrest, waste in government operations, and an unsettled peace. Inevitably, the incumbent party received the blame for all of this.

Even on the League issue, Cox and the Democrats played into Republican hands. By stressing it, Cox gave the Republicans an emotionally charged weapon to use against him. Despite the difficulty in securing unity in their own ranks on this question, all Republicans could condemn what was known—and the Wilson League was known. By identifying with the Wilson League completely, Cox severely limited his own freedom of action and became the recipient of most of the anti-League animosity formerly reserved only for Wilson.

In assessing the final Republican victory in 1920, it has often been claimed that the League issue was the primary downfall of the Democrats. This was a favorite refrain of anti-League stalwarts like Lodge, Borah, and Johnson. But historians have disagreed on how important this issue, as compared with others, really was. There is, for example, no way of knowing how many voted for the Republicans believing that this would ultimately lead to League membership and how many voted for them thinking it would prevent acceptance altogether. One thing is certain. A vote for the Republicans was a vote against the Democrats, and the Democrats represented the party of Wilson. A vote for the Republicans was clearly a vote *against* Wilson and his administration, whether it related to the League or to other social, economic, and political factors.

A vote for the Republicans was also, in most instances, a vote *for* the Republican candidate, Warren Harding. The conclusion often drawn is that Harding was simply the mindless beneficiary of favorable voter sentiment. But the setting of the 1920 campaign, the personalities of the candidates, and the nature of the issues make Harding's contributions especially significant. Harding aroused no animosities. He seemingly represented a return to national balance and sanity. He preached conciliation, moderation, cooperation, and recovery. While economic liberals were horrified by his conservative views on the tariff and finance, a nation in the midst of a severe depression regarded such opinions as pertinent and logical. His call for tax reductions and government economy appeared sound to a society still suffering from high wartime taxes and excessive government expenditures. His rather naïve appeals for industrial peace and for better labor-management relations seemed particularly timely in a period of widespread strikes and labor turmoil. His remarks concerning lynching appealed to a group just then migrating in increasing numbers from the South and beginning to exercise real political power in certain northern urban communities. By his various promises and his calm demeanor, and in many other ways, Harding successfully wooed businessmen, rank-and-file laborers, white-collar workers, housewives, and especially farmers, who, thoroughly fed up with Wilson, voted in droves for the Ohio senator.

With its candidate thus projecting an attractive and constructive image, the Republican party seemed far preferable to most citizens in 1920. Hence, the Great Mandate of that year was not an endorsement by default, nor was it merely a product of that amorphous factor called "the times." The Republicans and Harding won decisively on basic issues; they did not wrest responsibility for governing the country from their Democratic opponents by means of chicanery, intrigue, or money. Wilsonian liberalism had failed, and the Democrats could not expect reendorsement in the person of James Cox or anyone else. Cleverly sensing the political trends, the Republicans, mainly through the efforts of their candidate, successfully identified with the nation's longing for the twin blessings of peace and prosperity. Harding was not engaging in mere campaign rhetoric when, in his "normalcy" speech, he told the country precisely what it wanted to hear. William Gibbs McAdoo might later claim that such Harding utterances "left the impression of an army of pompous phrases moving over the landscape in search of an idea." [21] But McAdoo and other Democrats failed to realize that one such "pompous phrase," because of its universal appeal, was worth more in the currency of American politics than any number of truly wise observations. The single word "normalcy," especially, caught on. During the campaign Harding defined it thus: "By 'normalcy' I don't mean the old order, but a regular steady order of things. I mean normal procedure, the natural way, without excess." [22]

Few Americans in 1920 could quarrel with this sentiment. And when the Republicans managed simultaneously to convert Harding's "normalcy" into a synonym for prosperity and an antonym for Wilsonism, they became invincible.

21. William G. McAdoo, *Crowded Years: The Reminiscences of William G. McAdoo* (Boston, 1931), 388–89.
22. New York *Times,* July 21, 1920, p. 7.

2

Anatomy of an Administration—Harding Style

〰〰〰〰〰〰〰〰〰〰〰〰〰〰〰〰〰〰〰〰

IN MID-FEBRUARY 1921, after a day of roaming through the virtually empty offices of the White House, newspaperman Edward G. Lowry remarked that it appeared as though the government had gone out of business, that everything was "all unmarked and unadorned waiting what may come." [1] In the last days before the March 4 inauguration of Warren Harding, the Wilson administration indeed performed its caretaker chores almost somnambulistically. Its existence had obviously outlived its usefulness, and there seemed to be few mourning its impending demise.

The political coalition that had sustained Wilson's philosophy of progressivism before 1917 began crumbling with the onset of the war and collapsed completely in the postwar era. Intellectuals, progressives, liberals, and the reform-minded middle class found their former common bonds disintegrating in the face of wartime exigencies and disappearing altogether under the pressure of postwar emotionalism and economic selfishness. Held together somewhat longer than anticipated by an appeal to wartime patriotism, these elements by 1920 could no

1. Edward G. Lowry, "Before the Curtain Rises," *New Republic,* XXV, No. 325 (February 23, 1921), 374.

longer coalesce around either a common cause or a common personality.[2]

The war also had a profound effect on the structure and operation of the Wilson government, especially the executive branch. The pyramiding wartime bureaucracy overwhelmed what was left of the Jeffersonian orientation of Wilsonian liberalism. Such new civilian war agencies as the United States Shipping Board, the War Industries Board, the War Trade Board, the Railroad Administration, the Fuel Administration, and the Food Administration were far more compatible in both theory and practice with the national planning concepts of Herbert Croly and Theodore Roosevelt's New Nationalism than with the original spirit of the New Freedom. Wilson himself was at first uncomfortable with this wartime development and with the rapid and bewildering expansion of federal power it brought. Still, as wartime leader, he accepted such changes as being necessary for final victory. As an advocate of a strong presidency, Wilson ultimately embraced the burgeoning wartime bureaucracy as a valuable instrument in translating executive desire into quick unilateral action.

If Wilson was master of this system during the war, he became its major postwar victim. He ignored the necessity for adequate postwar planning and a controlled bureaucratic demobilization and reorganization. When the most crucial of the wartime agencies were dissolved, Wilson provided no substitutes for the interim exercise of power or decision-making, and the ensuing vacuum was never filled. His subsequent illness provided a convenient excuse for glossing over this failure in foresight. But even before his stroke, Wilson had shown signs of being unable to adjust to changing postwar circumstances as well as to adapt his liberal philosophy to postwar needs. His penchant for diplomatic secrecy, his manipulations with respect to the results of the Versailles Conference, his attempts to bypass or ride

2. Arthur S. Link, "What Happened to the Progressive Movement in the 1920's?," *AHR*, LXIV, No. 4 (July 1959), 833–51, discusses the question of the Wilson coalition and its disintegration.

roughshod over Congress, and his disinclination to compromise —all seemed to place him in an increasingly unfavorable, and even dictatorial, light.

What the pressures of war and the demands of the postwar era started, Wilson's illness completed. This event, more than any other, sent shock waves through his administration. After his stroke, he was kept in strict isolation by Mrs. Wilson and his physician, Admiral Cary T. Grayson, and was initially unable to exercise any decision-making functions at all. When this condition persisted, his administration simply foundered. Heavily dependent on his direct supervision and control, his cabinet and the other important members of the executive branch found themselves without adequate guidance or direction. Strong men are often wary of strong subordinates, and Wilson was no exception. He had not habitually surrounded himself with leaders in their own right. As a result, during his illness the piloting of the administration fell into the hands of those who were not prepared to assume independent roles. The aging vice-president, Thomas R. Marshall, was a nonentity and could not fill the gap. One cabinet officer, Secretary of State Robert Lansing, tried, but he was later removed for having made the attempt. Others, such as Attorney General A. Mitchell Palmer and Postmaster General Albert S. Burleson, also sought to fill the vacuum, but their activities were more destructive than beneficial in the long run. In brief, the cabinet's erratic response to the President's illness, its general lack of unity, and its incredible ineptness attested both to the caliber of the executive system in the last years of the Wilson administration and to its excessive reliance on the existence of one man.

For the first half of the last seventeen months of Wilson's second term, Mrs. Wilson (née Edith Bolling) was the closest thing the United States had to a chief executive. She, Admiral Grayson, and Joseph Tumulty screened all matters brought to the President's attention and allowed only those whom they endorsed to see him personally. During that period, this so-called bedroom circle permitted not one cabinet official to talk to Wilson. Indeed, Mrs. Wilson arranged for the replacement of two cabinet officers (one of them being Lansing) without the new appointees' seeing the President at all. When Wilson finally did return to part-time activity, he was unwilling to stop the disastrous drift in his administration. Instead, he spent his time brooding over the League of Nations defeat, heaping vindictiveness on his subordinates, and dreaming of running for a third term.[3]

With this background, Harding's assumption of power on March 4, 1921, was welcomed because it presaged a return to the proper functioning of government and an active struggle to restore prosperity. Further, the accession of the Republicans to power was expected to end the Wilson-style "one-man" rule and substitute a more balanced division of executive responsibility. With Harding's inauguration, there was indeed a shift in the temper, tempo, and emphasis of government. It is often mentioned that laughter quickly replaced the hushed silence of the Wilson sickroom, that flowers appeared again in the White House lawn, that garden parties were reinstituted, and that the gates to the White House grounds were thrown open. But these were merely surface manifestations of a much more significant development—a drastic alteration in the internal relationships of the executive branch of government and in the specific role played by the executive. Again, as in the outcome of the campaign of 1920, Harding's personality contributed greatly to this change.

In contrast with the cold and unapproachable Wilson, Harding had a magnetic quality that made both men and women like him. Charming and gregarious, he easily identified with people and they with him. Even his habits and vices marked him as an extremely likable and convivial personality—he drank an occasional highball, used tobacco in all forms, liked to play cards, loved children and dogs, and had a passion for golf.[4] Harding was listed by Irwin H. ("Ike") Hoover, chief usher at

3. Again, for the best analysis of Wilson's last days, see Smith, *When the Cheering Stopped, passim.*
4. For a fuller description of Harding's physical characteristics and personality, see Murray, *The Harding Era,* 114–23. Public controversy over Harding's drinking and card playing did not arise until after his death. At that time, his drinking habits were grossly exaggerated, as were the circumstances surrounding his card playing.

the White House for many years, as second only to Theodore Roosevelt in human interest and next to Lincoln in humaneness. Yet, unlike Roosevelt, Harding displayed little egotism and, like Lincoln, possessed a simple humility that was generally attractive.

Harding was perhaps best known for his friendliness and generosity. These two traits were extensions of his gregarious nature and also reflected his dislike of disharmony and contention. In both his private and his public life, he regarded compromise and conciliation as superior to argument and disagreement. Disagreement forestalled the resolution to problems while compromise enhanced it. Likewise, argument prevented the making of friends while conciliation aided it. Harding had a compulsive need for friends. Later critics attributed this compulsion to his small-town background, to his allegedly having Negro blood, to an abnormal craving for recognition and acceptance, and to a disbelief in his own capabilities.[5] Whatever the cause, he always sought and enjoyed good fellowship whether he was in the Elks Club in Marion, in the state legislature in Columbus, in the Senate in Washington, or in the White House.

Loyalty also was an extremely important element in the Harding personality. An acquaintance once remarked: "He liked politicians for the reason that he loved dogs, because they were usually loyal to their friends." [6] To Harding, loyalty was not only a requirement for political self-preservation but necessary for a full and meaningful life. Unfortunately, under its mandate he too easily overlooked moral defects and was often indiscriminate in his personal contacts. While his fear of offending anyone, especially his friends, prompted him to grant their requests too readily, his emphasis on loyalty caused him to stand by them regardless of what they had done.

5. Although the charge of Negro blood was an old myth, a recent biographer, Francis Russell, in *The Shadow of Blooming Grove: Warren Harding in His Times* (New York, 1968), builds his whole thesis around it.

6. Mark Sullivan, *Our Times: The United States, 1900–1925* (New York, 1935), VI, 102, n. 10.

However, it was the quality of Harding's mind and his attitude toward the presidential office more than these personal traits that ultimately determined his effectiveness as chief executive. Wilson once said that Harding had a "bungalow mind," and H. L. Mencken, offended by the syntax of Harding's speeches and his fondness for alliteration, claimed he possessed only a mediocre intelligence.[7] In a sense this was true. Harding revealed only limited vision and frequently succumbed to the requirements of political expediency. He tended to give pat answers rather than to think problems through. Actually, Harding had a good mind, but it was undisciplined. He was most comfortable in the realm of clichés and maxims, and left it to others to supply the necessary intellectual content.

Whatever his intellectual limitations, Harding was a hardworking president. After his first several months on the job, he rarely retired before midnight and was at his desk at 8 A.M. The press often commented on his work habits, Mark Sullivan writing in 1922: "In the mere prosaic quality of capacity for hard work, Harding is extraordinary." [8] Indeed, he worked harder as president than either Wilson or Roosevelt and twice as hard as Taft. He claimed that he had to work hard in order to compensate for his limited capabilities, and he hoped that diligence would counterbalance his weaknesses. He openly admitted that he could never match Wilson's brilliance or Roosevelt's drive. He would have to make his mark in another way. With considerable insight, he once remarked to a reporter for the New York *World:* "I cannot hope to be one of the great presidents, but perhaps I may be remembered as one of the best loved." [9]

7. Harding's speeches were not as bad as Mencken and certain others claimed, but they did contain remnants of turn-of-the-century Fourth of July oratory. The New York *Times,* for example, thought Harding's style was "excellent." "Mr. Harding is not writing for the super-fine weighers of verbs and adjectives," said the *Times,* "but for the men and women who see in his expressions their own ideas, and are truly happy to meet them." New York *Times,* April 24, 1921, Section II, p. 2.

8. Mark Sullivan, *The Great Adventure at Washington: The Story of the Conference* (New York, 1922), 225.

9. Charles Michelson, *The Ghost Talks* (New York, 1944), 229.

The impression often is that Harding was a hopeless dund-
erhead in the White House, that he had no coordinated thoughts
concerning the presidency, and that all he could do was fall
back on being "loved." This impression is much too simplified.
Harding's desire to be loved certainly did not qualify him as a
great political philosopher, nor did it help him to be a forceful
leader. But then, Harding at first gave no evidence of wanting
to be a dynamic leader. He actively shunned the idea of the
president's being an initiator and prime mover in governmental
affairs. He held in his mind the image of Wilson and his struggle
over the League as a clear example of the pitfalls that lay along
that path. It is significant that Harding had as his presidential
idol William McKinley, not Theodore Roosevelt. Indeed, Harding had earlier opposed Roosevelt and his belief in a strong president as a grave danger to the Republican party. From
Harding's point of view, Roosevelt, had he been in the White
House, would have made just as much a botch of settling the
peace and handling postwar problems as Wilson had done.

Harding was basically suspicious of presidential power and
disliked the thought of exercising it. Enemies were made
through the exercise of power, and enemies did not contribute
to political peace and tranquillity. Harding believed that if
presidential power had to be used, it should be used within well-
defined limits and with great restraint. He believed deeply in the
separation of powers in the American governmental system and
in the essential interdependence of the executive, legislative,
and judicial branches. More than once he declared that he did
not regard the presidency as superior to the other two, nor did
he believe that the president should exercise a monitoring function over them. Presidential authority was a constitutional
grant that was neither open-ended nor to be expanded by whim
or by elastic interpretation.

Harding did not regard the president as the mystical em-
bodiment of the will of the people. The president was not a
composite representative of all factions or all political and economic groups, nor was he the spokesman for any particular
political or economic interest. In Harding's view, the president

was not even necessarily the foremost leader in his own party. True wisdom and leadership in program development, for example, might rest with others rather than with the president. For this reason, Harding consistently talked about the need to rely on and consult with the "best minds" his party had to offer. Harding's humility undoubtedly would not permit him to regard himself as the most knowledgeable person on any given subject. However, he did not believe that any president, even Wilson, was sufficiently intelligent to act as the sole agent in careful decision-making. The discriminating executive would always depend on the "best minds," and then submit their collective judgment to over-all party review.

To Harding, the president's major function was to act as facilitator and compromiser, adjudicator and political counselor. He was to bring the "best minds" together, moderate their discussions, and supply the conciliatory spirit that would adjust diverse points of view. In implementing the resultant political program, the president was to ascertain that it represented majority feeling, then surrender it into friendly congressional hands with the assurance of broad party support. The outcome would be easily defendable at the polls, since it would represent a collective party action and not the effort of an oligarchy or of one man. This, felt Harding, was in keeping with the requirements of the democratic process. Under such circumstances, the president would be free to arbitrate political disputes, ride above inter-party and intra-party turmoil, and serve as the repository of good will for the entire political system.

To a large extent, Harding saw the office of president itself as a ceremonial one and that of a figurehead. One of the aspects of the presidency that he liked most was the pomp and ceremony connected with the post. Despite his basic humility, he relished the deference paid to the position and he enjoyed the various social activities surrounding it. But even these personal and rather selfish reactions grew out of his other beliefs. Harding could not conceive of a president's being paid national respect if, as he once said, the chief executive entered the political arena like an armed gladiator. Only a president who was loved could properly retain the public faith and be a symbol of national pride and confidence.

The first test of Harding's beliefs came in the selection of his cabinet, where he thought the "best minds" in any administration ought to be concentrated. Unlike most presidents, Harding wanted his cabinet selections to include, as much as possible, the intellectual and administrative leaders of the party. Each, he felt, should be closely identified with the area of endeavor to which he was appointed (e.g., business, agriculture, and so on) and have the respect of those who were important in that area. Together, these men would represent a reservoir of talent and information upon which he could rely in fashioning his normalcy program.

Much nonsense has been written about the selection of the Harding cabinet. It is common knowledge that there was wide consultation on cabinet positions and that the Old Guard, in particular, screened all candidates carefully. It is also well known that there was pressure from conservative elements to construct a cabinet that would not offend powerful business interests. What is not so commonly known is the role Harding played in the final selection process and how often he deviated from Old Guard and conservative preferences. Indeed, he rapidly discovered that he did not always wish to be merely a rubber stamp for the "collective wisdom" of the party or of any particular group in it, and that to attract the "best minds" to his administration he sometimes had to exercise his presidential prerogatives.[10]

The appointment of his secretary of state offers a case in point. Contrary to later claims, Harding never seriously considered anyone other than Charles Evans Hughes, senior party statesman and internationally known jurist, for this position. He offered it to him on December 10, 1920, when the New Yorker appeared in Marion as one of Harding's first official post-elec-

10. For the circumstances surrounding the selection of each of the cabinet members, see Robert K. Murray, "President Harding and His Cabinet," *Ohio History*, LXXV, Nos. 2–3 (spring-summer, 1966), 108–25.

tion visitors. However, the formal announcement of this appointment—the first regarding a cabinet position—was not made until mid-February 1921.[11] In the meantime, press speculation and rumors reached dizzy heights as "irreconcilables" such as Borah and Johnson, and Old Guard stalwarts like Knox and Penrose, filled the air with the names of potential candidates. Every conceivable possibility was presented, with Hughes being quickly eliminated because of his pro-League sentiments. But not by Harding. He had made his decision and he stuck by it, even though it obviously ran counter to the wishes of some of his oldest Senate friends.

Another appointment that reflected a strong Harding preference was that of Henry Wallace as secretary of agriculture.[12] One of the best-known agriculturalists in the country because of his editorship of *Wallace's Farmer,* Wallace not only had acted as Harding's farm adviser during the campaign but had helped write the Republican farm plank of 1920. However, he was detested by Old Guard conservatives because of his condemnatory wartime editorials on the malpractices of meat packers and food processors. Hence, he was rejected by them as cabinet material. But Harding thought otherwise and, despite vigorous protests, Wallace joined Hughes on the cabinet list.

An even more ticklish situation developed concerning Herbert Hoover. From the outset, Harding was attracted to Hoover as a cabinet member. However, the Old Guard and other elements in the party lived in fear of Hoover, regarding him as too internationally-minded, too independent politically, and too ambitious to be acceptable. Senator Frank B. Brandegee, an Old Guard poker friend, bluntly told Harding, "Hoover gives most of us gooseflesh," and others, such as Johnson and Lodge, heartily agreed. Hoover was also eyed with suspicion by Harry Daugherty, who nevertheless was told by Harding, "The more I

11. Acceptance letter is Hughes to WGH, December 13, 1920, Charles E. Hughes Papers (LC), Box 4A, folder "1920."
12. The original letter suggesting the post to Wallace was written even before the election. WGH to Wallace, November 1, 1920, HP, Box 535, folder 4197–1, item 243803.

consider him the more do I think well of him, [and] inasmuch as I have the responsibility to assume, I think my judgment must be trusted in the matter." [13] Thus, despite the fact that the consultation process clearly pointed to candidates other than Hoover, in early February Harding offered him the post of secretary of commerce. To the accompaniment of loud grumbling, particularly from Old Guard quarters, public announcement of Hoover's acceptance was made on February 24.[14]

Hoover's selection as secretary of commerce was closely connected with that of Andrew W. Mellon as secretary of the treasury. Mellon was not Harding's first choice for the treasury post. Charles G. Dawes, an Illinois banker, had that honor. But Easterners, and Wall Street in particular, were wary of the Midwesterner Dawes. As a compromise possibility, Senators Knox and Penrose mentioned to Harding their fellow Pennsylvanian, Pittsburgh millionaire Andrew Mellon. Since Knox and Penrose were known to be among the chief leaders in the stop-Hoover faction, Harding seized the opportunity to resolve two problems at once, and indicated that he might be swayed in Mellon's favor if their attacks on Hoover ceased. When they reluctantly agreed, Mellon was chosen.[15] A blend of pure chance, cold calculation, compromise, and political shrewdness, this selection was cabinet-making at its best.

While all four of these selections dovetailed with Harding's own desire to appoint the "best minds," four other cabinet appointments represented the normal surrender to political expediency. Since he had no strong feelings about these particular positions, Harding easily succumbed to the various consultative pressures and merely accepted what the winnowing process turned up. Still, in view of his "best minds" theory, he should have been less compliant. As it was, these four selections are ample proof that a broad interchange of views often results in

13. WGH to HMD, February 9, 1921, HP, Box 368, folder 2601–1, items 174897–900.

14. Hoover's acceptance is in telegram, Hoover to WGH, February 23, 1921, HHP, Box AK I–7.

15. Daugherty's account of this episode is in his *The Inside Story of the Harding Tragedy* (New York, 1932), 92–100.

mediocrity or worse. Political and geographic requirements pointed ultimately to the former Massachusetts senator John Weeks, Harding's business adviser during the campaign, as secretary of war. The post of secretary of labor went to James J. Davis, a onetime iron puddler who currently was better known for his lodge work as director-general of the Loyal Order of Moose. Will Hays was named postmaster general, though he actually coveted Hoover's position as secretary of commerce. Finally, the post of secretary of the navy was given to Edwin L. Denby, a relatively unknown former congressman and auto-mobile manufacturer.

The two remaining cabinet slots were filled according to a criterion entirely apart from either the consultative or the "best minds" principles, and indicated that friendship was still of great importance to Harding. From the beginning he insisted that at least two cabinet positions be reserved for his loyal friends. Al-bert Fall was thus named secretary of the interior simply be-cause Harding liked him. A former western marshal and Rough Rider, Fall had occupied a seat close to Harding's in the Senate and had enjoyed many a poker session with the new president. Fall's appointment was actually a convenient marriage of Hard-ing's desire to reward a friend and his recognition of geographic considerations. Fall was from New Mexico, and Interior usually went to a Westerner. Fall's anti-conservation views played no part in his selection, and later charges that he was named as a result of secret deals made with oil interests at the 1920 Re-publican convention were without foundation. Moreover, at the time of his selection there was no opposition to him on moral grounds, and, except for cries of anguish from a few conserva-tionists, his appointment was accepted with equanimity.[16]

Harry Daugherty's appointment as attorney general was also based exclusively on friendship. In this case, Harding not only refused to conduct a wide search for a "best mind" but stood openly and unabashed against the expressed will of his party. From the moment he suggested Daugherty, there were

16. Shaw to R. B. Harris, November 19, 1933, Ray Baker Harris Papers (OHSL), Box 3, folder 4, describing Fall's selection.

shouts of protest from virtually every quarter. Daugherty's shady political past made such objections inevitable. But Harding was unmoved. As early as mid-December 1920, he replied to a disapproving Senator Wadsworth: "I have told him that he can have any place in my Cabinet he wants, outside of Secretary of State. He tells me that he wants to be Attorney General and by God he will be Attorney General!" [17] Daugherty's appointment, announced publicly on February 21, had certain merits that were overlooked in the continuing uproar. He was a shrewd lawyer and more competent than many appointees to the post of attorney general. Moreover, he was an outstanding political trouble shooter and was of tremendous potential benefit to the administration in matters of party patronage. But as we will later see, subsequent events would cast grave doubt on Daugherty's *actual* value both to the administration and to the nation.

During and immediately after the oil and Justice Department scandals in 1923–24, these various cabinet selections were widely deprecated. Critics such as the *New Republic* and the *Nation* then spoke of Hughes and Hoover as mere "deodorizers" for Daugherty and Fall. In 1921, however, the press and most political observers, among them Mark Sullivan, greeted the cabinet as "one of the strongest groups of presidential advisors and department heads in a generation." [18] Even as late as 1944, despite intervening scandals, Charles Michelson, a journalist and long-time observer of Washington events, admitted, "Harding had possibly the highest-grade cabinet of modern years." [19] Ironically, the specific selections that made that cabinet both the best and the worst in modern times resulted from Harding's independent action and judgment rather

17. Wadsworth to R. B. Harris, June 20, 1938, Harris Papers, Box 2, folder 6. Before 1920, Daugherty was known mainly for his lobbying activities in Ohio and his high-pressure actions on behalf of wealthy corporation clients.

18. Mark Sullivan, "The Men of the Cabinet," *World's Work,* LXII, No. 1 (May 1921), 81.

19. Michelson, *The Ghost Talks,* 231.

than from the consultative process and over-all party review he so highly prized.

Harding had assumed that the mere gathering together of diverse and outstanding cabinet talent would produce a successful political program and immediate beneficial results. He was quickly disappointed. He found that his "best minds"—Hughes, Hoover, Wallace, and Mellon—did not react well to collective consultation and preferred to deal unilaterally and individually with him. From the beginning, therefore, he was presented with a developing executive relationship that a strong president would have purposely contrived. Indeed, cabinet meetings in the early years of normalcy were largely perfunctory and not the seminal discussions that Harding had expected. He tried not to monopolize cabinet debate as Wilson had done, and he encouraged cabinet participation. But few matters of importance were ever settled by the cabinet collectively, and most important decisions were reached outside the group by the President and the individual secretary concerned.

Hence, Harding became much more a factor in the decision-making process than he would have liked. To compensate, he often acquiesced unquestioningly in what a cabinet officer wished to do. As a result, the success or failure of various parts of the administration's normalcy program depended largely on the zeal and talent of the cabinet member involved. To a marked degree, Harding permitted each secretary to operate his department and set its guidelines as he saw fit. Unlike Wilson, he did not use his cabinet officers as errand boys, nor did he intrude on the organizational affairs of their departments. Departmental bureaucracies were allowed to function and be staffed as each cabinet official determined. Where a department head was an avowed spoilsman, like Daugherty, Harding only rarely intervened to prevent wholesale firings and straight-line party appointments. But if a department head was a believer in civil service, like Mellon, Harding supported his retention policies to the limit.

One criticism leveled against the Harding administration

was that the President was too much under the influence of his cabinet appointees. This was partially true. However, to state the fact too bluntly is to misjudge the unique nature of Harding's relationship with his cabinet. Most presidents did not regard their cabinets as the spawning ground for administration programs or ideas. They preferred instead to use ad hoc groups, such as the Kitchen Cabinet or the Brain Trust. During the early normalcy years, cabinet members themselves generated much of the administration's thrust and direction. This development had Harding's approval and was fully in keeping with his views on the sharing of executive responsibility.

It was expected that Fall and Daugherty, the two personal friends of the President, would exercise considerable influence over normalcy policies and enjoy wide latitude in running their individual bailiwicks. Daugherty always did dominate the Justice Department, and he maintained direct and speedy access to the throne. But his influence began to diminish by the spring of 1923 because of his ill health and the attacks made on him by Congress. His forte was campaign and election strategy, but he was out of his depth in program development and he knew it. Harding relied heavily on him for the former but largely ignored him in connection with the latter. Fall, in turn, kept in close contact with the President during the first year. By early 1922, their contacts markedly declined as rumors spread that Fall was dissatisfied with the growing importance of Hughes and Hoover in the cabinet.[20] By late 1922, the President's attitude toward the New Mexican had definitely cooled and his influence had reached the vanishing point.

Harding increasingly turned to Hoover and Hughes and, in certain matters, to Wallace and Mellon for the generation of ideas and administration guidance.[21] These were the men who, along with Harding, were primarily responsible for the specific acts and measures that fleshed out the philosophy of normalcy.

20. New York *Times,* January 22, 1922, Section III, p. 6.
21. Examples of presidential contact with these cabinet officers are found throughout HP. For Harding-Hoover correspondence in a concentrated form, see HHP, Box 1–I/242; 1–I/243; 1–I/244.

In matters of finance and fiscal policy, the key figure was Mellon. On almost all important economic questions, Harding, as well as the other cabinet officers, generally followed Mellon's advice. There were some differences among them. Harding, for example, was not as big-business oriented as Mellon, nor did he subscribe fully to Mellon's "save the rich" tax philosophies. But he, like the others, was content to let Mellon carry the financial ball.

Mellon was not close to anyone in the administration. Certainly his personal relationship with Harding was not intimate. Slight, frail, and seedy in appearance, Mellon did not have the expansive kind of personality that appealed to Harding. One well-preserved myth has it that the financier exercised great personal influence over the President. This was untrue. In cabinet meetings Mellon said almost nothing and never spoke on non-financial matters. But when he did choose to speak, especially on taxes or the tariff, all cabinet members, as well as the President, listened carefully, not because of the force of his arguments or his great wealth but because of a common conservative orientation they all shared. In short, Mellon was their spokesman, not their persuader.

On agricultural policy, Wallace was the administration's leader. Sensitive concerning his prerogatives and volatile in temper, he was brusque in his relations with other members of the cabinet. He was most compatible with Hughes, with whom he often played golf. His intensely partisan approach to agriculture ruffled feathers and led him into violent differences with his colleagues. His frequent arguments with Fall over conservation and his constant haggling with Hoover over matters of departmental jurisdiction marked him as being essentially parochial.

Harding liked Wallace, and the two were good friends. Wallace was an amiable companion at both golf and poker and, like Harding, sometimes chewed tobacco. More important, his views regarding agriculture closely coincided with those of the President. Harding strongly agreed with Wallace's desire to increase farm exports, raise tariff duties on agricultural items, conduct scientific cost studies, pass laws protecting farm cooperatives, improve the federal farm-loan system, and increase farmer representation on federal boards and commissions. But he differed from his secretary in refusing to consider farmers a special group to be subsidized directly if necessary by the federal treasury.

Herbert Hoover was clearly one of the most creative forces in the Harding cabinet. Unlike other cabinet officials, who minded their own department's business, the Secretary of Commerce was "assistant secretary" of everything else. He was the all-round expert, a fact often mentioned in the contemporary press. On finance, it was Mellon "and Hoover"; on labor problems, it was Davis "and Hoover"; on agriculture, it was Wallace "and Hoover." Yet Hoover's relations with other members of the cabinet were neither close nor especially friendly. In their reaction to him, resentment and admiration went hand in hand. Hoover was probably closer to Hughes than to any other cabinet member, but they were not friends. It was always "Mr. Hoover" and "Mr. Hughes." Perhaps their stiff personalities would not permit greater intimacy. In any case, Hughes was more pleased by a compliment from Hoover than from anyone else except Harding, and Hoover believed that Hughes was the most able man in the cabinet next to himself.

President Harding remained a consistent champion of Hoover throughout. Hoover's brand of "rugged individualism" appealed to the President, and his notion that each individual should "be given the chance and stimulation for development of the best with which he has been endowed" supplemented the President's own beliefs. Moreover, Hoover's view of government as an umpire rather than a policeman in the economic game was fully compatible with Harding's own ideas. Both men agreed that the administration should promote government-business cooperation and maintain an economic atmosphere in which industry could flourish.

Harding's official contact with Hoover was greater than with any other cabinet member except Hughes. He deeply valued Hoover's opinions, and many a Harding-to-Hoover letter ended with the sentence, "I will await your frank advice on the subject." Hoover, in turn, needed and relied heavily on Harding's protection. To the time of his death, Harding steadfastly backed his secretary of commerce and held him in highest esteem. He once remarked to E. Mont Reily, "Reily, do you know, taking Herbert Hoover up one side and down the other, and taking into consideration the knowledge he has of things generally, I believe he's the smartest 'gink' I know." [22]

But it was Hughes who was the most important and imposing figure in the cabinet. Dignified and widely respected, Hughes imparted to the entire administration an aura of solidity that no other contemporary statesman could have contributed. In this regard, the relationship between Hughes and Harding after 1921 was significant. Where Wilson had dominated his secretaries of state, Harding permitted Hughes free rein. Like the later John Foster Dulles under President Eisenhower, Hughes under Harding formulated and executed administration foreign policy. Although some critics later claimed that this was necessary because Harding was totally ignorant of foreign affairs, evidence shows it was not true; Harding gave Hughes this freedom by choice, not by default.

Because the two men possessed such contrasting personalities, there were often rumors of differences between them. Periodically, it was reported that Hughes was about to resign, but Harding would never have thought of dismissing Hughes, and Hughes would not have wished to resign. Hughes had a peculiar affection for Harding, and the President treated Hughes with great respect. Hoover later claimed that Hughes actually frightened Harding.[23] If that was so, it was not apparent from their correspondence or their personal contacts. Hughes relied on Harding for executive support and for his knowledge of the inner workings of the Senate; Harding left the running of the State Department to Hughes.

In the last analysis, it was Harding himself who was the

22. E. Mont Reily, "Years of Confusion," unpublished manuscript (OHSL), 264.
23. Herbert Hoover, *The Memoirs of Herbert Hoover: The Cabinet and the Presidency, 1920–1933* (New York, 1952), II, 36.

central figure in his own cabinet, because he fused the independent talents, especially of his "best minds," into a constructive political whole. Only a president with Harding's moderating influence could have prevented the egos of these cabinet members from clashing and escalating into damaging feuds, and only a chief executive with Harding's particular qualities could have retained their collective allegiance and respect. In addition, more than any of his "best minds," Harding was a sensitive and clever political animal. His knowledge of the American psyche was uncanny and proved invaluable to the ultimate success of his cabinet officers' various plans and proposals. The dignified Hughes, the impersonal Hoover, the combative Wallace, and the silent Mellon needed Harding to supply the human warmth and deft political touch they lacked.

While president, Harding was sincere in attempting to make the executive branch, burdened with increasing functions and responsibilities, more workable and more responsive to national needs. Certainly his system was in marked contrast with the Wilson "one-man" orientation. But it also differed greatly from what came later. Indeed, Harding was the last president to rely exclusively on constitutionally designated officials in his handling of the executive branch. Beginning with Hoover, and especially under Franklin Roosevelt, the administrative hierarchy was increasingly composed of special presidential assistants and advisers, and the cabinet was again relegated to a subordinate policy-making position.

Whatever their specific role in the development of American governmental structuring, Harding and his cabinet quickly accomplished the most immediate task before them—restoring direction and vigor to the executive branch of government. In virtually every department there was evidence of a new vitality and sense of purpose. This fact rapidly communicated itself to the entire federal bureaucracy and dispelled the malaise that during the last Wilson days had infected not only the highest decision-making levels but the lower echelons as well. Hays began an ambitious reorganization of the Post Office. Weeks initiated needed reforms in the War Department. Fall brought a number of administrative improvements to Interior. Even Daugherty effected some long overdue changes in the Attorney General's office. But it was in the major areas of concern— foreign affairs, agriculture, business, and fiscal matters—that there was the greatest activity and evidence of movement. With Harding's help, Hughes began to achieve a radical turnabout in the disastrous congressional-executive battle that had ruined Wilson's hopes for a lasting peace. Mellon launched an immediate drive to reduce government expenditures as a necessary step in the return to prosperity. Hoover began to convert the largely inactive Commerce Department into a beehive of pro-business activity. And Wallace, relying on Harding to prevent agricultural interests from being overrun by pro-business enthusiasm, set about reestablishing the "rights of farmers."

Although this executive system provided thrust once again and was an important achievement, it would not be an unqualified success. While the "best minds" would continue to function admirably, obvious mediocrity in such areas as Labor and the Navy would seriously impair the administration's effectiveness. Moreover, Harding's penchant for rewarding loyalty as represented by the appointments of Fall and Daugherty would overshadow many of the admirable contributions of the "best minds" and present the administration with difficulties. Further, contrary to Harding's belief that selection of the "best minds" would inevitably lead to other important results, these did not materialize. As we will presently see, this particular development did not restore "normal procedure, the natural way" or cause politics to be conducted rationally and "without excess." It would not, as Harding had hoped, bring about political stability or assure easy acceptance of the normalcy program. It would not prevent the continuation of intense political partisanship and congressional wrangling. And finally, because of the permissiveness inherent in this arrangement of collective executive responsibility, it would not provide the necessary supervision to forestall corruption or the firmness to deal with it when it appeared.

3

Congressional Politics— Drift and Mastery

〰〰〰〰〰〰〰〰〰〰〰〰〰〰〰〰〰〰〰〰〰〰〰〰〰

"NOW, BOB, BE GOOD," said Harding as he patted Senator LaFollette on the shoulder. "I'll be busy making you be good," LaFollette retorted.[1] This short but significant exchange occurred on December 6, 1920, at the opening of the last session of the 66th Congress, when Harding appeared briefly to bid farewell to his Senate colleagues before taking over the presidency. As LaFollette's words betrayed, Harding's legacy from Wilson included not only an executive branch in confusion, a foreign policy in chaos, and a domestic economy in shambles, but an angry, suspicious, and rebellious Congress.

Since 1918, Congress had been the scene of disquieting power struggles and rising antagonisms. Some upsurge in congressional dissension could reasonably have been expected to follow the termination of the war. But the nature of the congressional conflicts after 1918 transcended the mere manifestation of politics suddenly freed from the fetters of wartime unity. Actually, there had never been any real lapse in political partisanship during the war, and the post–1918 development was for the most part a continuation and intensification of an anti–New Freedom spirit that had been building up for some time.[2]

However, there was one significant new feature in the post–

1. Fola and Belle C. LaFollette, *Robert M. LaFollette* (New York, 1953), II, 1020.
2. The best coverage of Congress during the wartime period is in Seward W. Livermore, *Politics Is Adjourned: Woodrow Wilson and the War Congress, 1916–18* (Middletown, Conn., 1966).

1918 situation. Because of stunning Republican victories in the congressional elections of 1918, the Democrats had no semblance of a public mandate for the difficult task of liquidating the war and making the peace. In the 1918 elections, not only did the Republicans succeed to majority control of Congress, but some of the most vociferous anti–New Freedom and anti-Wilson spokesmen were placed in key positions of responsibility. For example, Penrose became chairman of the powerful Senate Finance Committee, while Lodge took over as chairman of the Senate Foreign Relations Committee. These men simultaneously opposed anything that seemed to perpetuate the New Freedom and loudly called for higher tariffs, lower taxes, and greater efficiency in government—issues they had been attempting to capitalize on since pre-war days. By making the defeat of such individuals and a resounding administration re-endorsement the foremost considerations in 1918, President Wilson certainly did not help his or his party's cause. Thereafter, like Andrew Johnson in 1866, he had to live with the unhappy consequences. In longevity alone, those consequences were rather severe, since the disaster of 1918 began a decline in Democratic power that extended not only into but through the 1920s.

Although the Democratic party in Congress was visibly shaken by the 1918 election, its leadership was already badly divided over the postwar character and direction of the New Freedom program. A noticeable conservative trend had set in among Democratic congressional leaders as early as 1916 and had grown during the intervening war years. Some of these leaders, especially from the nonprogressive regions of the South and the business areas of the North, had expressed increasing distress over the wartime expansion in executive powers and had viewed with disfavor the possible peacetime continuance of the civilian war agencies. Hence, at the close of the war, many of these Democrats joined with Republicans to demand, and then hail, the rapid demise of most of the wartime boards. At the same time, certain Democratic senators began to match their Republican counterparts in calling for the restoration of a prewar balance between Congress and the president. These men were uneasy at the prospect of continued executive "superiority" and often unwittingly helped their Republican opponents force executive-legislative showdowns in which Congress could reassert itself. In some respects, the subsequent League struggle was an outgrowth of this over-all postwar concern of Congress to "regain" its former authority.

In addition to intensifying the legislative-executive struggle, the League fight had a tremendously debilitating effect on congressional Democrats. Congress is, after all, an arena of political combat where compromise is the most useful and effective weapon. Yet Wilson, by his uncompromising stand in the League fight, arbitrarily denied this weapon to his followers. In view of the fact that the Republican party then controlled the Senate, Wilson's stubbornness was clearly an act of political folly. By his obduracy, Wilson reduced his two chief congressional lieutenants, Senators Underwood and Hitchcock, to impotence and totally eliminated their ability to maneuver. More than once these pro-League leaders begged to be released from Wilson's no-compromise commitment, but they always failed. In the end, not only the President but his entire party suffered a humiliating defeat.

Wilson's illness completed the Democratic disintegration. Its long-range effect on the Democrats in Congress was no less disastrous than on the functioning of the executive branch. Only twice were Democratic congressional leaders allowed to see the President during his illness, and each time they came away without any suggestions as to how to keep the party unified and how to attack the nation's mounting problems. As a result, a virtual shutdown occurred in Democratic-sponsored congressional activity, since no new departures, new programs, or new ideas were presented. Democratic congressional leaders were obviously afraid to take any new step without the President's specific approval. Meanwhile, they remained confused as to what direction Wilson wished the postwar New Freedom to take. By his avoidance of postwar planning, Wilson had not provided any format for his congressional lieutenants to follow.

This confusion and this vacuum in leadership ultimately caused party control, which had been sustained remarkably well through the League fight, to collapse. By 1920–21, the Democratic party was rapidly disintegrating into a confederation of sectional interest groups, which argued angrily over such divisive matters as railroad legislation, the tariff, and taxes. What unity the Democrats preserved rested largely on their emotional reaction to the increasingly powerful Republicans.

The Republicans enjoyed the Democrats' discomfort. Before they secured congressional control in 1918, they shot at the Democrats from the sidelines to the extent that general support for wartime policies would permit. But with the end of the war and their victory in the 1918 elections, they boldly attacked the Wilson administration on all fronts. Claiming legitimacy by virtue of the 1918 endorsement, the Republicans in Congress demanded a halt to further New Freedom experimentation and expansion of presidential power. Moreover, they sought the immediate dismantling of the entire Democratic-sponsored wartime regulatory and control structure. Anxious to reestablish Republican supremacy not only in Congress but in the White House as well, Republican congressional leaders maintained an uncooperative attitude throughout 1919–21, dragging their feet on all except Republican-endorsed legislation, thus making congressional progress on postwar problems of any kind impossible. By 1921, even if the Democrats had presented Congress with a postwar program of substance, Republican intransigency would have postponed its consideration or killed it.

If the League struggle had a debilitating effect on congressional Democrats, it invigorated the Republicans. True, the Republicans were divided on this particular issue; however, a general anti-Wilson animus tended to hold the various Republican factions together. More significant, the intense acrimony of the League debate and President Wilson's obstinacy polarized the parties more than might otherwise have been the case and, in the end, the Republicans appeared to most observers to emerge victorious as a group. Republican animosity toward Wilson was immeasurably heightened by the President's pro-League activities, and this emboldened certain elements in the party, specifically the violently anti-Wilson group led by Lodge, to exercise increasing influence over the party as a whole. Such elements held not only Wilson but the presidency itself in deepening disdain and consciously sought to undermine presidential influence in all areas, not merely in foreign affairs.

Wilson's illness and ensuing postwar difficulties produced a feeling of impending success among these anti-Wilson forces as well as among Republicans in general. Inflation, unemployment, business depression, and social turmoil proved to be especially profitable issues for congressional Republicans. They could dwell on the problems without bearing the responsibility for the solutions as long as the White House remained in Democratic hands. Frankly, the chief goal of the Republican congressional leadership between 1919 and March 4, 1921, was not to find answers but to emphasize the poor state of existing conditions. Constructive politics might demand a more rational Republican response, but smart politics dictated inaction. Consequently, on only minor matters, such as appropriations, conservation legislation, and prohibition enforcement, did the Republicans allow congressional action to be taken.[3]

Ironically, when Republican success was finally achieved in the election of 1920, the Republicans in Congress were ill prepared to capitalize on it. Their opposition had been primarily negative, and they had not developed a program or blueprint for action. Their strong anti-Wilson prejudices had prevented them from adopting a positive approach to many of the nation's most serious problems. For a time, the League struggle so dominated congressional thinking that solutions had been easily ignored. More important, beyond demanding that all wartime regulatory controls cease, the Republican congressional leadership had said little about the party's postwar goals. Out of the White House for eight years, the party at that time had no single leader to look to for guidance and, except for its anti-Wilson

3. For congressional matters in 1918–20, see Frederic L. Paxson, *Postwar Years: Normalcy, 1918–1923* (Berkeley, 1948), 40–197.

attitudes and its general desire for higher tariffs and lower taxes, it seemingly had no sense of purpose.

Almost by default, the Republican senatorial leadership attempted to speak for the party before Harding's inauguration in 1921. This group had received broad national exposure during the League fight and was thought by the public to possess a certain cohesiveness. Indeed, one of the most interesting results of the League struggle was the emergence of the Senate, at least in the eyes of the public, as the most potent force in American political life. To some extent, this Senate image held throughout the 1920s. In the Senate, the Republican party possessed a number of well-known spokesmen, each of whom sponsored well-publicized projects or championed certain issues. Some were avowed business conservatives, but some were not. As a result, these men had much difficulty working together as a unit. In essence, they represented only the specific wishes of their particular patrons or constituents rather than some overall political program. Perhaps this was inevitable, since the nation itself was sharply divided over most issues by 1920, each citizen or interest group advocating that action which would do it the least harm or benefit it most. In 1920, congressional Republicans, both in the Senate and in the House, merely reflected the general public desire to secure personal postwar advantages.

One major change that most observers expected to see from the Wilson years was a *détente* in the growing executive-congressional confrontation and closer cooperation between the White House and Capitol Hill. Harding, after all, had been a member of Congress and knew intimately its inner workings. Besides, the Senate "oligarchy" myth surrounding his nomination fed the belief that he would be a president highly acceptable to Congress. Harding, of course, held most of the views associated with the conservative Republican element in the Senate—lower taxes, higher tariffs, greater efficiency in government, and so on. But his friendliness and his proclivity for compromise also made him fully intend to get on well with Congress as a whole and remain on good terms with all factions. In this regard, his convictions concerning the president's proper relationship to Congress were significant. Harding believed that the president should be aware of the full range of congressional opinion on national problems and consult closely with congressional leaders about the administration's program and its enactment. He considered the congressional input in the developmental process second only in importance to that of the cabinet. As a result, Harding did confer frequently with congressional leaders, and they supplied him with some of the substance that ultimately became the normalcy program. Where Wilson had called congressional leaders to the White House mainly on special occasions, Harding issued them a standing invitation, and they often appeared voluntarily to air their views. He sought to encourage a free exchange of ideas in other ways, sometimes going to the Capitol to lunch with his former Senate colleagues, hoping thereby to better understand them and to have them better understand him. This "fraternization" seemed to some critics to indicate a dependence of the executive on Congress, which they did not like. But for Harding such contact was desirable in order to keep the lines of communication open.

In the matter of program implementation, there was no question about the President's philosophy. Harding believed that it was the responsibility of the party's leaders in Congress, not the president, to guide the administration's program safely through that body. Congressional leaders were to isolate pockets of resistance, use their persuasion and authority to win stragglers over, and, if all else failed, apply sanctions to hold the membership in line. Harding considered maverick or insurgent activity by Republicans a political sin. He desired that such defections be held to a minimum and was willing to help persuade such individuals to follow majority party opinion. But his disinclination to offend, as well as his belief in the adjudicatory function of the presidential office, prevented him from accepting the idea of executive reprisals. The sin of insurgency should be handled by the party itself.

These presidential views concerning legislative-executive relationships were a part of what Harding meant when he defined normalcy as "normal procedure, the natural way, without excess." In essence, his attitudes pointed to a relatively weak and nonaggressive presidency, a situation extremely palatable to most congressmen. Congressional leaders expected Harding to be weak. They *wanted* him to be weak. In their quest to restore the balance between Congress and the executive, they looked upon Harding as a helpmeet. Senate Republicans, in particular, contemplated breathing easier with Harding in the White House. Even before Harding's inauguration, Senator Lodge made it clear that he now anticipated a return to "consitutional government," which frankly meant less presidential meddling in legislative affairs. In this hope he was joined not only by the Old Guard but by insurgent Republicans such as LaFollette. In their own way, all of these men wanted to make Harding "be good."

The Republican-dominated 67th Congress, which was called into special session in April 1921, was certainly designed to put all these theories to the test. Partisanship was its hallmark. It suffered not only from the partisanship of Republicans versus Democrats but from the undisciplined and unpredictable partisanship of competing intra-party vested-interest groups. As a whole, Congress was still smarting from the bitterness of the League fight, and many members, Republicans and Democrats alike, had been so poisoned by that experience that they remained unable to cooperate on virtually any issue. In particular, there were the "irreconcilables" in both parties, like shock-maned Senator Borah (Rep., Idaho) and acerbic Senator James A. Reed (Dem., Missouri), who refused to support any proposal that hinted even vaguely at a modification in their isolationist stand.[4] Simultaneously, there was the Old

4. The 67th Congress contained twelve of the original sixteen "irreconcilables." Of the twelve, eleven were Republicans. Besides Borah, there were Robert M. LaFollette (Wisconsin), Frank B. Brandegee (Connecticut), George H. Moses (New Hampshire), Medill McCormick (Illinois), George W. Norris (Nebraska), Hiram Johnson (California), Joseph I. France (Maryland), Philander C. Knox (Pennsylvania), Bert M. Fernald (Maine), and Miles Poindexter (Washington).

Guard in the Senate and their counterparts in the House, led by such Republican leaders as Senator Penrose (Pennsylvania) and Representative Joseph W. Fordney (Michigan), ardent pro-business champions who sought special advantages for the business community.[5] At the same time, there was the southern Democratic bloc, headed by Representative John N. ("Cactus Jack") Garner of Texas and velvet-tongued Byron P. ("Pat") Harrison of Mississippi, which strongly supported favorable regional legislation but opposed almost everything else.[6] Representatives from large metropolitan areas, such as Adolph J. Sabath (Dem., Illinois) and Isaac Siegel (Rep., New York), were just now surfacing as a definable group and were also upsetting party loyalties.[7]

Of all these divisive factors, however, none was so significant as the farm bloc. Cutting across all party lines, but primarily affecting the Republicans, this group symbolized the farmers' desire to force the government to help them out of the agricultural depression. Derisively nicknamed "the sons of the wild jackass" because of their constant "braying" about rural distress, the bloc was led in the Senate by William S. Kenyon

5. Counted in the ranks of the Old Guard were Frank Brandegee (Connecticut), Lewis Ball (Delaware), Medill McCormick (Illinois), Joseph E. Watson (Indiana), Harry S. New (Indiana), Henry Cabot Lodge (Massachusetts), Joseph S. Frelinghuysen (New Jersey), Boies Penrose (Pennsylvania), James W. Wadsworth (New York), William M. Calder (New York), Philander C. Knox (Pennsylvania), Walter Edge (New Jersey), Joseph I. France (Maryland), Frederick Hale (Maine), and Reed Smoot (Utah).

6. Besides Harrison, the southern bloc in the Senate had as its core J. Thomas Heflin (Alabama), Thaddeus H. Caraway (Arkansas), Joseph T. Robinson (Arkansas), Thomas E. Watson (Georgia), John S. Williams (Mississippi), Furnifold M. Simmons (North Carolina), and Kenneth D. McKellar (Tennessee). In the House its leaders, besides Garner, were George Huddleston (Alabama), William B. Bankhead (Alabama), Charles R. Crisp (Georgia), Alben W. Barkley (Kentucky), John E. Rankin (Mississippi), Claude Kitchin (North Carolina), Edward W. Pou (North Carolina), and Sam Rayburn (Texas).

7. Fiorello LaGuardia would ultimately become the chief spokesman for this group. However, he was not in the 67th Congress but would be in the 68th and 69th Congresses.

(Rep., Iowa) and in the House by Lester J. Dickinson (Rep., Iowa). Comprising a loose combination of midwestern, western, and southern agricultural votes, it usually acted as a brake on the activities of the pro-business group but sometimes held the balance of power on other critical issues.[8] Indeed, with the farm bloc in the picture, the Republican majorities indicated by the congressional election results in 1920 appeared rather meaningless. Only rarely in either house was the Republican party able to muster its overwhelming number of votes. Usually the Republican vote was badly splintered, with farm-bloc members adopting a highly independent stance. Joined from time to time by the southern Democratic element led by Garner and Harrison, this farm group created havoc in Republican ranks.

No less greedy, no less aggressive, and no less ruthless than any other pressure group in pursuing advantages for its constituents, this farm bloc would prove that the bulk of the early opposition to normalcy policies arose not from a desire to revive the spirit of progressivism or return to the days of Wilson but to profit economically from the postwar readjustments. Farm spokesmen from both House and Senate would speak of lofty principles and condemn their business opponents for callousness and reactionary thinking, but aside from their personal political philosophies, they had as their immediate goal the passage of legislation beneficial to the farmer, and often *only* to the farmer. In this regard, the harangues and exhortations of men like Senators George W. Norris (Rep., Nebraska), Peter Norbeck (Rep., South Dakota), and even LaFollette rang

8. Besides Kenyon, among the farm-bloc members of the Senate were Robert LaFollette (Rep., Wisconsin), George Norris (Rep., Nebraska), Arthur Capper (Rep., Kansas), Edwin F. Ladd (Rep., North Dakota), Peter Norbeck (Rep., South Dakota), Frank B. Kellogg (Rep., Minnesota), Robert N. Stanfield (Rep., Oregon), Charles L. McNary (Rep., Oregon), John W. Harreld (Rep., Oklahoma), Henry F. Ashurst (Dem., Arizona), Claude A. Swanson (Dem., Virginia), Morris Sheppard (Dem., Texas), and John B. Kendrick (Dem., Wyoming). Besides Dickinson, other House leaders of the bloc, who could sometimes muster as many as 90 to 100 votes, were George Huddleston (Dem., Alabama), Charles B. Timberlake (Rep., Colorado), George M. Young (Rep., North Dakota), Willis C. Hawley (Rep., Oregon), Lindley H. Hadley (Rep., Washington), and James A. Frear (Rep., Wisconsin).

no truer or less selfish than those of their business counterparts. Farm-bloc rhetoric notwithstanding, self-serving politics in the early 1920s was universal.

It was to this Congress with its congeries of special interests that Harding directed his first official message on April 12, 1921. His address was a product of wide consultation with cabinet officials and congressional leaders, including the farm bloc, and defined the challenges facing his normalcy administration. Suggesting that Congress should take up domestic problems first, Harding mentioned the need for an increase in the tariff and lower taxes, greater economy in government, a law providing for a national budget system, the construction of a great merchant marine, a reduction in railway rates, new farm-credit legislation, tighter immigration controls, the creation of a system of national highways, the enactment of a maternity bill, immediate development and effective regulation of aviation and radio, the passage of an anti-lynching law, and the creation of a Department of Public Welfare. With respect to foreign affairs, he expressed hope for world disarmament and for an association of nations "binding us in conference and cooperation for the prevention of war," but declared that the United States should not enter the Versailles League. He further stated that peace treaties should be arranged rapidly with all former enemy states and that an orderly funding of war debts should be undertaken.[9]

This speech was one of the best of Harding's career. By it he set the perimeters of what came to be called the "normalcy program" and at last gave his party a definite mission. Although the speech was the result of collective consultation, it clearly enhanced his personal image and inevitably injected him into the legislative arena. Not only did it reveal that Harding was aware of all the major problems confronting the nation, but it indicated that he was more advanced in his thinking about the range of difficulties facing the country than were many congressmen who were currently worried only about their own

9. Warren G. Harding, *Speeches as President,* "Address of the President of the United States, April 12, 1921" (OHSL), 3–19.

specific concerns. Not unexpectedly, the weakest part of the speech involved the League of Nations and foreign affairs. Still, Harding showed a desire to restore economic ties and improve relations with all nations and, to that extent at least, sought to place the United States again in a world setting.

Congress received this speech with surprise. There was something in it that appealed to everyone. Yet there was also something in it that offended everyone. Progressives were antagonized by Harding's conservative tax and tariff proposals; conservatives were nervous about his reference to new regulatory legislation and lower railroad rates. Pro-Leaguers were disheartened by his comments on the League; "irreconcilables" were angered by his renewed talk about an association of nations. Hence, although the address was hailed in the press as "a fresh start," because of its breadth and content it raised immediate questions about whether or not it could be implemented.

Harding's address presented such a comprehensive program that it made congressional confusion over priorities a virtual certainty. Already, in the late Wilson years, congressional Republicans had argued among themselves over what problems to attack first but had never reached any conclusions. Anxious not to be drawn into an intra-party controversy, Harding had decided not to announce any mandatory guidelines in his special message, indicating only that in his opinion a reduction in taxes and an increase in the tariff were the two most critical items. He frankly hoped that Congress would establish its own timetable. But congressional leaders, representing diverse economic interests, remained unable to agree on a plan of action. Spokesmen of the farm bloc, such as Norris, Norbeck, and LaFollette, demanded that immediate attention be given to a new tariff to raise duties on agricultural commodities, while pro-business champions, such as Penrose and Fordney, protested that tax reductions should come first.

Faced with this impasse at the very beginning of his tenure, Harding rapidly discovered that he could not remain completely aloof from legislative matters. Indeed, unlike most presidents, he never really enjoyed a honeymoon with Congress. Having no desire to participate vigorously in congressional affairs, he nevertheless did not want Congress to waste time in bickering or to succumb to the tendency to drift. To arrange a compromise between the contending factions seemed to Harding to offer the best chance of generating momentum without involving the presidency too deeply. Hence, he suggested a loose priority formula, which was finally agreed upon, whereby the House Ways and Means Committee would discuss a new tariff while the Senate Finance Committee would begin tax hearings. Even so, for nearly three months the special session of the 67th Congress continued to quibble over priority matters while the White House stood anxiously by.

Meanwhile, some progress was made in enacting the normalcy program. Realizing that writing a new permanent tariff would take time and that the farmer needed immediate relief, both houses rapidly agreed to an Emergency Tariff, which was signed by Harding on May 27, 1921. This brief "Two-Inch Law" temporarily provided for higher duties on wheat, corn, meat, wool, and sugar. Although the measure passed by a wide margin, debates on it offered a portent of things to come. In particular, the rebellious mood of many midwestern Republican farm members was underscored by their warnings that the eastern manufacturer had better "wake up to the fact" that the western producer deserved just as much attention from the government as he did. Farmers, they said, would not remain docile forever.[10]

Less controversial was a new immigration law, which was quickly passed. The foremost congressional champion of immigration restriction was Albert Johnson, a Republican from the state of Washington and the chairman of the House Committee on Immigration. He and some of his like-minded House colleagues, such as Thomas L. Blanton (Dem., Texas) and Riley J. Wilson (Dem., Louisiana), actually desired immigration suspension. But William P. Dillingham (Rep., Vermont), who was responsible for shepherding an immigration measure through the

10. *Congressional Record,* 67th Congress, 1st Session, 327, 335, 1308, 3084, sample debates.

Senate, succeeded in getting agreement on strict limitation instead. Called the "Per Centum Law," this act continued the
traditional exclusion of Asiatics and restricted other immigration annually to 3 percent of a country's nationals residing in
the United States in 1910. The measure was endorsed by the
House 276 to 33 and passed the Senate with only one negative vote. Designed to discriminate against migrants from southern and southeastern Europe, the act effectively reduced the
number of entering aliens from 805,228 in 1920 to 309,556 in
1921–22.[11]

One further normalcy suggestion received rapid endorsement—the creation of a national budget. The administration's
desire to reduce government expenditures and inject business
methods into government operations met with almost universal
congressional approval. Consequently, Congress hurried through
the so-called Budget and Accounting Act, which Harding signed
on June 10, 1921. This law created a budget bureau in the
Treasury Department but made it directly responsible to the
president. Under the law, the president was required to prepare
an annual budget with the aid of the bureau and submit it to
Congress for approval.[12] Harding immediately selected Charles
Dawes as the budget director, and in a whirlwind performance
the Illinois banker swiftly made budget control and a reduction
in government expenses a reality.[13]

The speedy passage of these three measures—an emergency
tariff, a strict immigration law, and a budget act—did not eliminate the continuing priority struggle between congressional advocates of tax reductions and those who favored farm relief. It
did, however, force a shift in their tactics. Before the passage
of the "two-inch" Emergency Tariff, agricultural representatives
had been the main champions of a new permanent tariff, supporting this priority, at least partially, to forestall tax reductions
they feared would primarily benefit business. But as soon as the

11. *Ibid.,* 513, 516–18, 948–54, 1442–43, 1774, for debates and
final vote.
12. *Ibid.,* 1850–53, 1859.
13. For Dawes's appointment and his activities, see Charles Dawes,
The First Year of the Budget of the United States (New York, 1923).

Emergency Tariff removed the urgency of the tariff issue, farm champions quickly switched to other demands. To the dismay and anger of tax reductionists, rural representatives now warned that, despite the presidential priority formula and the passage of the Emergency Tariff, further pro-agricultural legislation would have to be considered before tax reform.

In late May and June, therefore, a whole series of agricultural bills were introduced in both houses by farm-bloc members, amid charges of betrayal from pro-business advocates. Backing this rural action was Secretary Wallace, who, believing that additional farm legislation should take precedence over tax reductions, opposed Mellon and business leaders on this issue. Wallace and Mellon naturally made the President the focal point of their disagreement as each sought to win his favor. Surprised by this turn of events, Harding at first insisted that his compromise formula be followed. But internal dissension in his own cabinet and the intransigency of congressional farm elements finally forced him to take a stand. Through Wallace, a conference was arranged with farm-bloc leaders in early July, and the White House promised to lend its support to the most important of the many farm proposals and push for their immediate enactment.

Between then and August 24, 1921, five agricultural measures were passed by Congress and signed by Harding. Four of these bills were relatively noncontroversial and were adopted without much difficulty. They were the Future Trading Act, the Packers and Stockyards Act, and two amendments to the Farm Loan Act. Secretary Wallace was the prime mover behind all these measures. The Future Trading Act (Capper-Tincher bill) was a reform law that more carefully regulated the grain exchanges by placing a prohibitive tax on speculative transactions involving "puts and calls," "bids," and "offers." The Packers and Stockyards Act prohibited interstate packers from manipulating or controlling prices and from resorting to other unfair or discriminatory practices. The two amendments to the Farm Loan Act augmented the capital of federal land banks, authorized an increase in the maximum size of rural loans, and raised the interest to the investor on farm-loan bonds without increasing the rate to the borrower.

The most controversial of the farm measures, and one which illustrated that differences of opinion existed among farm-bloc members themselves, was the fifth and last—the Emergency Agricultural Credits Act. This law was actually an administration substitute for the so-called Norris Farm Relief bill, which had been sponsored earlier by Senator Norris, who at the time was chairman of the Senate Committee on Agriculture and Forestry. More radical in his economic beliefs than most of his Republican farm colleagues, Norris was, as one observer described him, "the burr Nebraska delights in putting under the eastern saddle." A vigorous champion of rural interests and a farm-bloc kingpin, Norris had designed his measure to perform the dual function of giving food relief to Europe while eliminating farm surpluses at home. At the heart of his proposal was the creation of a government corporation to buy farm surpluses for cash and then sell them abroad for credit. The secretary of commerce was to act as the ex officio chairman of the governmental board established to run this corporation.

The farm bloc had greeted the Norris bill with approval. Senator Kenyon was particularly enthusiastic. Even Secretary Hoover, who would have been chairman of the proposed corporation, showed an interest in it. But Secretary Wallace approved neither of Norris's plan nor of Hoover's projected role in it. Taking his cue from his secretary of agriculture, Harding also indicated his opposition. Southern farm leaders from the cotton states announced that they too could not support it, because they feared the bill might aid the rehabilitation of European textile mills. Hoover, meanwhile, noting the trend of opinion, withdrew his tentative support.

In seeking an alternative to the Norris plan, Hoover, with the aid of Wallace, drafted the Emergency Agricultural Credits Act. This measure was then given to Senator Frank B. Kellogg (Rep., Minnesota), a moderate member of the farm block, who on July 26, in a tricky parliamentary maneuver, substituted the measure for the Norris proposal. Such subterfuge caused bitterness among the more radical bloc members, but the combined support of moderate farm-bloc senators and the backing of the administration resulted in final victory. Signed by Harding on August 24, 1921, the Emergency Agricultural Credits Act authorized the governmental purchase of paper secured by agricultural products from rural banks; the granting of loans for the breeding, fattening, and marketing of livestock; and the advancement of loans to farmers' cooperatives and to foreign purchasers of American farm commodities in order to stimulate trade.

All five of these agricultural laws were supported by the administration in good faith not only because it desired to help the depressed farmer but also because it hoped to clear the path for tax reform. Yet the farm bloc never admitted that these laws had firm administration backing, and, indeed, some bloc members (especially the more radical of them) made it appear that the administration had actually opposed them. No mention was ever made of the fact that the bloc's main difference with the administration was over the question of timing, and not about whether there should be remedial farm legislation. Hence, by the fall of 1921 a dangerous credibility gap had developed between Washington and the farmer, and the President and his aides were at a loss as to what to do about it. Even Wallace felt he had been betrayed and complained to anyone who would listen: "The fact of the matter is that people generally have not given [the administration] the credit to which it is entitled." [14]

The presidential green light for a consideration of the five farm measures finally signaled the beginning of serious deliberations on tax reductions. Appealing particularly to the business community, tax reform was regarded as absolutely essential to industrial recovery. Business leaders had hoped that as soon as the special session opened Harding would push for tax re-

14. For a complete coverage of the administration's aid to the farmer, see Murray, *The Harding Era,* 199–226. Wallace quotation is in Wallace to WGH, January 10, 1922, HP, Box 197, folder 227–2, item 93610.

lief, and they were dismayed when the President went along with the demands of the farm bloc instead.

If business leaders had reason to be disappointed in Harding's performance, they could not criticize Mellon's. From the beginning, the Secretary of the Treasury urged quick congressional tax action and argued against concessions to farm elements. Mellon first applied pressure on the Senate, but when that body proved unresponsive he shifted his attention to the House. In late July, after consideration of the five farm-relief bills had begun, the House Ways and Means Committee finally asked Mellon for his recommendations for changes in the existing revenue law. That law provided for a 4 percent tax on the first $4,000 of income and 8 percent on the remainder. Surtax rates climbed from 1 percent on incomes in excess of $5,000 to a maximum of 65 percent on incomes over $1 million. The corporation tax was 10 percent, and there was also an excess-profits tax. Mellon recommended that the excess-profits tax be repealed as of January 1, 1921, that the maximum surtax rate be reduced to 32 percent, that the general income tax rates of 4 and 8 percent be retained, and that the corporation tax be lowered if possible.

The House Ways and Means Committee was headed by Joseph Fordney. A wealthy, self-made businessman, he strongly favored Mellon's proposals. But he was opposed in his own committee by a determined southern-western bipartisan coalition composed of such diverse members as James. A. Frear (Rep., Wisconsin) and "Cactus Jack" Garner (Dem., Texas). This dissident group forced the committee, contrary to Fordney's and Mellon's wishes, to raise the corporation tax to 12.5 percent, increase the tax exemptions for low incomes, and raise the allowance for dependents. But it could not prevent the committee from agreeing to repeal the excess-profits tax as of January 1, 1921, and to set the maximum surtax rate at 32 percent as Mellon had recommended.

When this bill came to the House floor, it created a furor. Naturally, the most vociferous opposition came from Democratic members, particularly rural southern Democrats such as Ed-

ward W. Pou (North Carolina), John E. Rankin (Mississippi), and Garner (Texas), who vented their wrath on Republicans in general, Northerners in particular, and northeastern
Republicans specifically. Garner, especially, drew applause
from his Democratic colleagues when he ridiculed Mellon and
challenged him to a public debate on his "medieval" tax philosophies. But these Democrats did not fight alone. Farm elements generally, including numerous Republicans, condemned
the bill as a rich man's measure and claimed that it would
further fasten corporation control on the country. A few Republicans even matched Democrats in making dire prophecies
about the future if the bill were passed.[15]

To proponents of tax reform this reaction seemed outrageous—especially since they were holding their own tongues
while the last of the farm-relief bills were being debated and
passed. Admittedly, the major defect in the proposed tax bill
was the absence of extensive relief for those in the lower income
groups. But tax reductionists claimed that as a recovery measure the bill had much to commend it. Statistics showed that
the rich were currently diverting income into tax-free securities
and that the number of persons paying the highest surtax rates
was declining. Moreover, despite the concern of some in Congress for the "poor taxpayer," fewer than 28 percent of the nation's eligible voters, and fewer than 18 percent of those gain-
fully employed, had been required to file a return in 1920
—and not all of these had paid a tax.[16]

President Harding did not understand all the intricacies of
the tax situation. He was frankly startled by the vehemence of
the House tax debates and confused by the conflicting opinions.
He once confided to a friend, Judson C. Welliver: "I can't make
a damn thing out of this tax problem. I listen to one side and
they seem right, and then—God!—I talk to the other side, and

15. For sample debates, see *Congressional Record* 67th Congress, 1st Session, 5131–34.
16. Statistics are from NICB, *Tax Burdens and Exemptions*, Report No. 64 (New York, 1923), 29, Table 10; 119, Table 31; 128.

they seem just as right." [17] Faced with this dilemma, Harding again sought deliverance by compromise, hoping thereby to resolve some of the difficulty. He indicated to House Republican leaders that he would accept January 1, 1922, instead of January 1, 1921, as the repeal date for the excess-profits tax. But for the moment he stood by Mellon's original proposals on surtax rates. With this indication of some presidential malleability, House Republicans closed ranks, protected the measure from any further changes, and by a special parliamentary maneuver rushed the final product through in four days.

In the Senate, the situation was more complicated. Already, in July, farm-bloc senators had attempted to forestall Senate action on tax reductions by spearheading a drive to put consideration of a soldiers' bonus ahead of tax reform. It was a clever ploy. A soldiers' bonus was extremely popular and, at the moment, was about the only issue on which bipartisan senatorial support could be achieved. As was its custom, the administration reacted at first with soft words and appeals to reason. On July 6, Secretary Mellon sent a letter to the Senate urging it not to consider a bonus bill, at least until the question of tax revision was fully settled. The next day, Harding lunched with a number of his old Senate friends and personally requested them to delay action on a bonus and to concentrate on tax reform. But these attempts at persuasion were insufficient to stanch the flow of pro-bonus Senate sentiment. Clearly, despite White House objections, the Senate intended to go ahead with a bonus, thereby not only endangering tax reductions but undermining the administration's drive for a decline in government expenditures.

By midsummer of 1921, Harding was becoming painfully aware that he could not continually escape the unfortunate consequences of a divided party by using only persuasion, compromise, and conciliation. His reliance on these tactics was simply inadequate to keep the normalcy program on the track,

17. William A. White, *The Autobiography of William Allen White* (New York, 1946), 616, quoting Harding.

and he now faced the possibility of having to intervene directly in congressional affairs to get the necessary result. He did not relish such a prospect and would have liked to use another way. But, as he wrote in anguish to his close friend Malcolm Jennings, "I find I can not carry my pre-election ideals of an Executive keeping himself aloof from Congress." [18] Hence, on July 12, in a precedent-shattering move, Harding suddenly appeared before the Senate in person and, in a twenty-one-minute address, scolded it for being slow on tax revision. Demanding a new tax law at once, he expressed great sympathy for the bonus principle but predicted "disaster to the nation's finances" if one was enacted without proper funding. He concluded by saying that under current circumstances "no thoughtful person, possessed with all the facts," could recommend passage of a bonus.[19]

Harding's surprising intervention in Senate affairs and his unexpected firmness on tax revision came at a time when his stock was high—he had just announced the calling of the Washington Disarmament Conference. The public frankly liked this sudden display of executive authority and his "no nonsense" approach to the upper body. On the other hand, some senators, among them LaFollette and Borah, were incensed that the President should thus openly attack the Senate and its handling of legislative matters. To them, Harding's action was an unwarranted exercise of presidential power and reminiscent of Wilson's executive highhandedness. In the halls and the cloakrooms they privately expressed their anger, but publicly they had to keep quiet in view of popular and press acclaim for the President. Said the New York *Times:* "The people are with him. There is nothing for the Senate to do but to recommit the Bonus bill." [20]

On July 15, the Senate did agree to postpone consideration of the bonus bill. This midsummer altercation, however, did

18. WGH to Malcolm Jennings, July 14, 1921, HP, Box 699, folder 1, item 151332.
19. Harding, *Speeches as President,* "Address of the President of the United States to the Senate, July 12, 1921," *passim.*
20. New York *Times,* July 14, 1921, p. 14.

not put the Senate, especially pro-bonus and farm-bloc members, in the happiest frame of mind when it did finally, in September, take up the House tax bill. Violent debates on the matter first erupted in the Finance Committee, headed by Senator Penrose. Penrose, suffering from terminal cancer, undertook this tax struggle as his last legislative battle. Throughout, he acted as the administration's spokesman and served specifically as a channel for the expression of Mellon's views. Despite bitter southern and farm-bloc opposition, and under Penrose's ruthless prodding, the Finance Committee ultimately reendorsed the House (Mellon-sponsored) surtax rates and in a few instances even lowered them. But contrary to the desire of Penrose and Mellon, the Harding-sponsored and House-approved date of January 1, 1922, for the repeal of the excess-profits tax was retained.

On the Senate floor, the bill faced determined opposition. Some of it came from the Republican-dominated agricultural states of the Midwest, but, as in the House, the attack was spearheaded by the southern wing of the Democratic party. Furnifold M. Simmons (North Carolina), a minority member of the Finance Committee, opened the debate with a slashing denunciation of Mellon. He was soon joined by others such as Reed (Missouri), Harrison (Mississippi), J. Thomas Heflin (Alabama), Kenneth D. McKellar (Tennessee), and Thaddeus H. Caraway (Arkansas). More disconcerting was the fact that a number of Republican farm-bloc members rushed forward to help the bill's Democratic opponents. Borah, LaFollette, Norris, Norbeck, and Edwin F. Ladd (North Dakota) led the defections.

On November 7, after fifteen hours of acrimonious debate, the Senate finally passed its version, 38 to 23, and sent it to conference. It differed mainly from the House version in the matter of surtaxes, the Senate adopting a 50 percent maximum surtax rate rather than the House-approved 32 percent. In conference, a deadlock on surtaxes quickly arose. With no end to the impasse in sight, the White House was requested to suggest a compromise and, risking Mellon's displeasure, Harding approved a maximum rate of 40 percent. Ironically, when the conference measure with this amended rate was later reported to the two houses, the House surprisingly voted 201 to 173 to accept the Senate maximum rate of 50 percent rather than the presidentially approved lower figure. To support this action, ninety-four Republicans broke from their party leadership. Immediately thereafter, the Senate voted quick reendorsement of its own 50 percent rate, while angry parting shots were traded by administration supporters, farm-bloc members, and gleeful Democrats. In the end, only one Democrat (Edwin S. Broussard of Louisiana) joined with thirty-eight Republicans to vote for the bill. Six Republicans—Borah, LaFollette, Norris, Norbeck, George H. Moses (New Hampshire), and Ladd—were among the twenty-nine senators who voted against it. All but Moses were from western or farming states.[21]

The Revenue Act of 1921 was not at all what Mellon had wanted and was a much more equitable tax than he had proposed. Significantly, this new law was as much a disappointment to those who desired thorough tax revision as to those who wanted no change at all. Certainly it was no sellout to business, as some claimed. In the end, it contained some relief for everyone, rich and poor alike, and represented a typical product of compromise politics. Harding realized this, even if Mellon and his more extreme agrarian opponents did not, and happily signed the measure on the same day it was passed, November 23, claiming that it fulfilled his campaign promise of lower taxes. Tax savings in the first year under the law amounted to over $800 million.[22]

November 23, the day Harding signed the tax measure, was also the day the special session of the 67th Congress adjourned. More than eight months before, Harding had called it into being to deal with the many problems confronting the nation in the post-Wilson era. Torn by dissension and racked by regional and partisan feuding, this session had accomplished

21. *Congressional Record,* 67th Congress, 1st Session, 8175.
22. Roy G. and Gladys C. Blakey, *The Federal Income Tax* (New York, 1940), 218.

more in the domestic area than was first apparent. An emergency tariff to protect farm products and five important farm-relief measures had been passed, a Budget and Accounting Act had been put through, an emergency immigration bill had been endorsed, and tax reductions had been effected.

Throughout this session, the administration had achieved these goals by indulging the Republican congressional leadership and by giving it the widest possible latitude in handling normalcy proposals. Whether the suggestions had originated with cabinet officers (e.g., tax reductions), were the joint creation of cabinet officials and congressional leaders (e.g., remedial farm legislation), or sprang directly from congressional committees (e.g., the Per Centum Law), they were subjected to minimum executive manipulation and interference. Unquestionably, this low presidential pressure and the White House's willingness to consider congressional sensibilities facilitated the passage of these various proposals. On the other hand, this special session, except for tax reductions, saw only the least controversial portions of the normalcy program debated and passed. Even so, party disunity and a divided congressional leadership had already marred the congressional scene, and on one occasion—the bonus scare—the President had been forced against his principles to intervene. Although gratified and somewhat surprised by the favorable public reaction to this one intrusion, Harding still preferred compromise and persuasion to adjust legislative-executive differences. By the end of the special session, however, future prospects for the continued success of such tactics were not bright.

Strangely enough, the one area in which Congress and the administration cooperated most closely during this period was foreign affairs. Except for the "irreconcilables," Congress evidently was tired of fighting the executive branch on foreign-policy matters. More important, the Harding administration's middle-of-the-road approach to foreign affairs was obviously highly acceptable to the average congressman and to the general public. Congressional cooperation, therefore, was not extracted but was granted freely. For example, the two houses quickly agreed on a joint resolution (Porter-Knox) to end the war, and Harding signed it on July 2, 1921.[23] Subsequently, peace treaties with Germany, Austria, and Hungary were considered by the Senate and, despite some Democratic and "irreconcilable" opposition, were ratified.[24] The Senate also agreed to an administration request to wipe out a blot that had remained on United States–Colombian relations since the Panama revolution of 1903 by accepting a treaty with Colombia that included payment of $25 million as "heart balm" to recompense for our earlier actions.[25]

This surprising cooperation on foreign affairs, begun in the special session, continued throughout the Harding years. Subsequent major foreign-policy matters involving the White House and Congress were the disposition of the various Washington Disarmament Conference treaties and the endorsement of agreements concerning the funding of World War I debts. In the latter case, the administration bypassed an earlier strict congressional directive establishing harsh terms for the funding of all Allied war debts, and negotiated instead a much milder arrangement with the British. Despite some grumbling, the Senate ultimately accepted this action, 70 to 13, thereby canceling its earlier instructions and opening the way for the more lenient handling of all subsequent funding agreements.[26]

The Washington Disarmament Conference treaties provided the most spectacular example of congressional-executive cooperation. From the time the disarmament conference convened, in November 1921, until it adjourned, in February 1922, the administration nursed a fear that the Senate might not accept the results. Therefore certain precautions were taken. With Wilson's ill-fated League experience fresh in his mind, Harding allowed Hughes to conduct the negotiations, rather than undertake them himself. He also appointed Senators Lodge and Un-

23. *Congressional Record,* 67th Congress, 1st Session, 3299.
24. *Ibid.,* 6438–39.
25. *Ibid.,* 487.
26. Original instructions are in *Congressional Record,* 67th Congress, 2nd Session, 1978. Final agreement is in *Congressional Record,* 67th Congress, 4th Session, 3786.

derwood, the ranking Republican and Democratic members of the Senate Foreign Relations Committee, to the official United States delegation and gave them the joint responsibility of piloting the treaties through the Senate. Then, leaving nothing to chance, on February 10, 1922, he appeared before the Senate and submitted the treaties in person. Reminding the Senate that he had had occasion in the League fight "to learn of your very proper jealousy of the Senate's part in contracting foreign relationships," he nevertheless added, "I have come to know the viewpoint and inescapable responsibility of the Executive," and asked that the treaties be ratified quickly.[27]

Despite the fulminations of "irreconcilables" and the mischievous meddling of a few spiteful former pro-League Democrats, all the treaties were finally ratified, including the Four Power Treaty (which involved Pacific security), and the Five Power Naval Treaty (which limited naval tonnage). In the crucial final votes, only four Republicans sided with the opposition, while twelve Democrats crossed party lines to vote for the treaties. The four dissenting Republicans were all former "irreconcilables"—Borah, LaFollette, Hiram Johnson, and Joseph I. France (Maryland).[28]

The most significant result of this cooperation in the foreign area during the period 1921–23 was the removal of foreign affairs as a serious political factor. Where foreign policy had been a primary point of contention in the Wilson years, it played no such role in the early normalcy era. Domestic affairs were another matter. No sooner had the second session (December 5, 1921–September 22, 1922) got underway than the farm bloc again created trouble by demanding additional farm relief. Again, the administration sought to meet the bloc's demands. In February 1922, it supported the passage of the Capper-Volstead Act, which allowed any farm association, cor-

27. For a full discussion of Harding's specific role, see Murray, *The Harding Era,* 140–66. Quotation is from *Congressional Record,* 67th Congress, 2nd Session, 2392.

28. For sample debates on the treaties, see *Congressional Record,* 67th Congress, 2nd Session, 3786–97, 3895–98, 4079–80, 4315–20, 4496–97, 4540–44.

porate or otherwise, with or without capital stock, to be exempted from the operation of the antitrust laws. In March, it extended its farm-loan activities by making an extra $1.5 million available to farmers for the purchase of seed grain in areas of crop failure. Finally, just before the end of the second session in September, the administration endorsed the passage of a Grain Futures Act to replace the Future Trading Act of 1921, which had been invalidated by the Supreme Court as an illegal use of the taxing power. This new law accomplished the same purpose but was based on the interstate-commerce clause.

Despite such sympathetic administration action, the farm bloc never stopped its harassment. Not content merely to hold legislative hostages (such as tax revision) in order to gain its goals, it began to attack the prerogatives of the executive. This trend was most clearly revealed in a bloc proposal made shortly after the opening of the second session, which would have enjoined the President to name "a farmer" as an additional member to the Federal Reserve Board. Farm congressmen were convinced that inadequate agricultural representation on the Federal Reserve Board had helped trigger the farm depression of 1920—hence the need for additional "rural" appointments. However, in a move that was highly reminiscent of the radical Republicans in the post–Civil War era, the farm bloc also designed the proposal to weaken the president by limiting his appointive powers through a congressional directive.

Rather than fight, Harding once again resorted to compromise, hoping thereby to placate farm sentiment and at the same time to preserve executive freedom of action. On January 16, 1922, the day before the Senate was to vote on the Federal Reserve Board proposal, Harding called Kenyon and Kellogg, the two key farm-bloc members, to the White House and secured agreement on a substitute proposal that would not force him to name "a farmer" specifically but would provide for greater agricultural representation on the Federal Reserve Board. Bankers and the commercial community immediately charged Harding with having surrendered to the bloc, while metropolitan newspapers claimed that farmers had the President "on the run." But Harding played down the implied threat to executive power, told reporters that "no harm was done," and assured the business and financial communities that it was only reasonable for agricultural groups to seek equality with them on the Federal Reserve Board.[29]

Although most observers continued to believe that the farm bloc had forced a humiliating capitulation on the administration, events soon showed that Harding, by his malleability and his conciliatory attitude, was actually diluting the bloc's militancy. The most direct manifestation of this was the subsequent shift in bloc leadership. Senator Kenyon, the highly respected and independent leader of the bloc, had long coveted a federal judgeship. Harding knew of this interest, and on January 31, 1922, in the wake of the Federal Reserve Board compromise, suddenly nominated Kenyon as a circuit judge for the Eighth District. Farm-bloc members immediately concluded that the President took this action as a warning to the bloc that the president's appointing power was intact and that it could even be used to break up the bloc by removing its leader.

The charge was at least partially correct. Harding did not create Kenyon's desire for a judgeship, but he certainly did not waste tears over the bloc's misfortune in losing him, either. Like any good politician, Harding combined circumstance with coincidence and turned both to his advantage. Whatever the President's motives, one fact emerged. There was a marked decline in the prestige and effectiveness of the farm bloc as Kenyon's successor, moderate Arthur Capper, took over. Thus, by the end of the second session, in September 1922, the administration had simultaneously robbed the bloc of many of its major issues by simply granting them and deprived it of its most effective leader. In a sense, the administration was successfully neutralizing the bloc through kindness. Indeed, never again was the bloc so tightly knit or so unified in action. This proved especially frustrating for such members as Norris and LaFol-

29. WGH to Hays, January 17, 1922, HP, Box 130, folder 90–2, item 64174.

lette, who were engaged in trying to build an ever stronger
rural base from which to launch assaults on normalcy policies.
For a time, these men were still convinced that they were
succeeding. But, despite continued loud words and rural fireworks, the bloc's finest hour had been reached during the summer and fall of 1921, when it had blocked tax revision and had
forced a consideration of the five farm-relief measures instead.

Besides providing additional farm-relief, the second session
of the 67th Congress also wrestled with writing a new permanent tariff and sought to resolve the postponed soldiers'-
bonus question. Moreover, in February 1922, it was asked by
the administration to adopt a complicated system of ship subsidies. Of these three issues, the soldiers' bonus seemed the most
important to most congressmen while ship subsidies were of
primary concern to the administration. But tariff revision took
precedence over both on the congressional calendar.

The House had already acted on a permanent tariff. Shortly
after the "two-inch" Emergency Tariff was passed in May 1921,
the Ways and Means Committee worked out a permanent
scheme to replace the 1914 Underwood-Simmons Tariff by re-
instituting across-the-board high protective rates for both agriculture and industry. Passed by the House on July 21, 1921,
this measure (Fordney bill) had been sent to the Senate, where
it was hoped final action could be taken before the special session adjourned in November. However, farm-relief legislation,
foreign affairs (the peace treaties), and tax revision intruded on
the Senate's time and made quick consideration impossible.

In his State of the Union message at the opening of the
second session in December 1921, Harding singled out the tariff
for special attention and declared that because of his campaign
promise in 1920 the Republican party could not again go before the electorate with confidence until a new permanent law
was written. But by late 1921, Congress, especially the Senate,
was growing wary of the tariff problem. More and more legislators were adopting the opinion that it was foolhardy to write a
new permanent law so soon after the war. By late winter of
1922, even the administration began to waver. Many business

interests, however, badly wanted new tariff rates and regarded the administration's flagging vigor as another indication of its greater sensitivity to the needs of the rural sector than to those of the industrial community. As winter wore into spring and still there was no tariff action, ardent protectionists became increasingly vocal and deluged the White House as well as the Senate with pro-tariff mail.

In mid-April 1922, with business pressure mounting and the White House again indicating concern over the tariff delay, Senator Porter J. McCumber (Rep., North Dakota), successor to the deceased Penrose as chairman of the Senate Finance Committee, reported a tariff bill to the Senate floor that was considerably different from the House measure. The Senate version, according to McCumber, protected American industry without creating a Chinese Wall of duties, and incorporated numerous other salutary provisions, including a White House-endorsed plan for limited presidentially controlled rate flexibility. Despite McCumber's laudatory advertisement for this measure, the majority of Republican senators greeted it without enthusiasm. Congressional elections were not far off, and few Republican senators relished a tariff fight at this particular moment. The Indianapolis *News* correctly assessed Republican senatorial opinion when it said: "It is highly probable that many of them wish the bill had never been introduced or that, having been introduced, it could now be dropped." [30]

The chief reason for this lack of enthusiasm was the degree of party disunity that debates on a new tariff would undoubtedly disclose. Subsequent rate discussions did cause partisanship and regional and occupational greed to assume their most virulent form. The debates sometimes took on an aspect of sheer fantasy. Violent arguments ensued over the proper duties for shelled almonds, egg albumen, cocoa butter, soap, wallpaper, saddles, and hides. The confrontation between the farm bloc and business representatives was acrid. Farm spokesmen claimed agricultural rates were ridiculously low when compared with

30. Washington *Post,* May 19, 1922, p. 6, quoting the Indianapolis *News.*

those proposed for industry. Hence, they clamored for the highest possible duties, logrolling where necessary to get them. In their protection mania, rural representatives often engaged in economic lunacy. They demanded exceedingly high rates on those items the farmer exported, such as wheat (thus securing protection the farmer did not need), in exchange for high duties on manufactured items, such as clothes and building materials, which the farmer customarily bought. There was even bitter wrangling over the White House–sponsored flexibility provision. Still suspicious of executive power, many senators did not wish to allow the President any leeway in adjusting rates. Rural western and southern senators worried about what the granting of such power would mean.[31]

On August 19, the Senate finally passed the McCumber bill, 48 to 25, with more than a score of senators, half of them Republicans, refusing to vote. Sent to conference, this Senate bill was amalgamated with the earlier House (Fordney) measure by a committee composed of ten members drawn from the two bodies, including Fordney and McCumber. For a fortnight this group repeated in microcosm what had gone on in the Senate as a whole. The result was a fantastic hodgepodge of rates, many of which were devoid of economic significance. Both agricultural and industrial representatives jockeyed for protective preference, and factional bitterness markedly increased. When Senator Kellogg complained in the committee that many of the high industrial duties would be resented in the rural areas he represented and might even cause him to lose his seat, Representative Fordney retorted: "Well, I would rather see the Senate lose you than American industry suffer." [32]

When the resultant conference measure was reported to the House, there were immediate signs of dissatisfaction. On September 13, Representative Garner skillfully played rural Republicans off against their industrial colleagues and got the House to send the conference bill back to committee with in-

31. For sample debates on the tariff, see *Congressional Record,* 67th Congress, 2nd Session, 9914–31, 10985–94, 11597, 11603–27.
32. New York *Times,* September 10, 1922, p. 1, quoting Fordney.

structions to place potash fertilizer on the free list and eliminate the embargo on dye. When the conference report, thus amended, arrived in the House two days later, Garner again attempted to have it recommitted, this time to readjust the sugar schedules. Finally aware that the Democrats were merely stalling and purposely sowing further dissension in their ranks, the shattered Republican forces regrouped and sullenly adopted the measure, 210 to 90. Four days later, the Senate concluded its deliberations, but not before talkative Democratic senators like Harrison, Heflin, and Caraway repeatedly embarrassed Republican supporters by their sledge-hammer assaults on the conference bill. The final Senate vote was 43 to 28. Five Republicans— Borah, LaFollette, Irvine L. Lenroot (Wisconsin), Ralph H. Cameron (Arizona), and Albert B. Cummins (Iowa)—voted against, and two Democrats—Edwin Broussard and Joseph E. Ransdell, both of Louisiana—voted for. Again, more than a score of senators did not vote.[33]

After many months of patient waiting, President Harding signed the Fordney-McCumber bill into law on September 21, 1922. Aside from its flexibility provision, this tariff was of dubious value. As a constructive economic measure, it made little sense. It was merely a patchwork of expediency and economic greed. The tariff debates had rarely involved principle; there were no great clashes as in the past between high- and low-tariff advocates. It was simply a struggle between vested-interest groups for economic advantage. As the New York *Commercial* described it: "The tariff now represents the composite selfishness of the country." [34]

Politically, this tariff made even less sense. It further split an already divided Republican party and further decreased the ability of the party's leadership to maintain discipline. The tariff debates provided an environment in which economic, regional, class, occupational, and political divisions could be

33. For House action, see *Congressional Record,* 67th Congress, 2nd Session, 12717–18; for Senate, see *ibid.,* 12907.
34. "The Farmer and 'His' New Tariff," *Literary Digest,* LXXV, No. 1 (October 7, 1922), 13, quoting the New York *Commercial.*

exploited. The result was growing congressional anarchy. Throughout, Harding attempted to stick by his non-involvement principles and, except on the question of rate flexibility, indicated a willingness to accept whatever Congress would give. The President, along with most of his cabinet, persisted in the belief that the passage of almost any kind of permanent tariff was essential in view of the campaign promise made in 1920. Continued business support seemed to hinge on it. For that reason, Harding spoke of the Fordney-McCumber tariff as an administration "victory." But it was a Pyrrhic victory in that it left the political battlefield strewn with numerous Republican dead.

If the second session of the 67th Congress finally produced a new permanent tariff, it did not grant something even closer to the administration's heart—subsidies for the merchant marine. In the merchant marine field, the Harding administration had inherited a sorry situation. Corruption, waste, and inefficiency had surrounded the wartime building of merchant ships, and now, in the postwar period, the government was saddled with an obsolescent fleet suffering from high operational costs, the animosity of private shipping, and a world-wide shipping depression. To straighten out this mess, Harding appointed Albert Lasker, his 1920 campaign publicity director, chairman of the United States Shipping Board. Lasker tried various approaches to the problem, including selling the fleet to private owners at ridiculously low prices. When these efforts failed, he finally recommended, with Harding's full approval, a system of shipping subsidies.

On February 18, 1922, Harding unfolded this scheme in a special message to a joint session of Congress. Under the plan, a fund was to be created to aid private shippers in building new ships as well as in buying the existing wartime government fleet. Subsidies would be paid to private shippers on a sliding scale, depending on vessel speed and gross tonnage. Shippers were to be allowed a 10 percent annual profit, but any excess would be divided between the owners and the government until the amount of the subsidy was repaid. The estimated cost of the program was $30 million per year. In presenting this plan to Congress, Harding pointedly admonished:

We have voiced our concern for the good fortunes of agriculture, and it is right that we should. We have long proclaimed our interest in manufacturing, which is thoroughly sound, and helped make us what we are. . . . But we have ignored our merchant marine. The World War revealed our weakness, our unpreparedness for defense in war, our unreadiness for self-reliance in peace.[35]

Harding obviously saw nothing unusual in this subsidy proposal. He had always favored a strong merchant marine as essential to business health as well as to national greatness. He had therefore included it among his campaign promises of 1920. As for special privilege, he considered ship subsidies no different from the tariff for industry or farm-relief measures for agriculture. Certainly he never considered the proposal as anti-agriculture and was surprised when the opponents of the measure adopted this attitude.

It was already a divided and troubled Congress that in the spring of 1922 held joint hearings on the subsidy scheme, and as the hearings progressed lines began to harden on the President's proposal. Senator Wesley L. Jones, chairman of the Senate Commerce Committee, finally threw his weight behind it, along with many East Coast, West Coast, and Gulf Coast representatives. Senator Capper, however, announced his refusal to support it, and other farm-bloc members followed suit. They claimed that the proposal was designed to help the eastern seaboard and wealthy shipping interests at the expense of everyone else. Even within the administration some disagreement developed over the plan. Secretary Hoover endorsed it, as did Secretary Mellon. But Secretary Wallace expressed grave doubts about it and conducted a hit-and-run debate with Lasker concerning its merits.

35. Full text is in Harding, *Speeches as President*, "Address of the President of the United States, February 28, 1922," 1–11.

Because of the urgency of the situation and because of his deep feeling concerning the merchant marine, Harding was at last compelled to shelve his "hands-off" policy and enter the fight for ship subsidies. Again, he would have preferred to remain in the background, allowing the party leadership to handle the struggle. But the apathy, even hostility, of many Republican leaders toward the plan left him no alternative. As a result, throughout the spring the White House exerted increasing pressure to force ship subsidies upon Congress. At first, such pressure took the form of mild persuasion, but it rapidly escalated to a sharp demand. By May 26, Harding was writing Philip P. Campbell, chairman of the House Committee on Rules, that a prompt consideration of the subsidy proposal simply had to be arranged. He warned that if Congress failed to pass the bill before the end of the second session, he would "call Congress immediately in extraordinary session to especially consider it." A week later, on June 3, Harding called a White House conference to which he invited Campbell of the Rules Committee, Chairman Horace M. Towner of the Republican caucus, George W. Edmonds of the House Merchant Marine and Fisheries Committee, Floor Leader Frank W. Mondell, and Speaker Frederick H. Gillett to develop common strategy for the bill's passage. In response to his guests' pleas for postponement, Harding flatly stated that he wanted the subsidy bill "above everything else." [36]

These White House actions revealed a much more vigorous Harding than Congress had become accustomed to and indicated that his former behavior pattern was undergoing marked change. In the ship-subsidy case, he apparently was willing to risk open rebellion among congressional leaders to get his way. On June 12, Representative Mondell again argued with Harding over the wisdom of the move, pointing out that even if the House passed the bill, the Senate was unlikely to get around to it before the end of the session because of its current preoccupation with the tariff. On June 14, Harding replied that nothing

36. WGH to Campbell, May 26, 1922, HP, Box 147, folder 99–4, item 71792; New York *Times,* June 4, 1922, p. 1.

could dissuade him from pushing ahead. Two days later, Mondell wrote the President that because of his insistence the bill would be introduced, but that the latest head count revealed it would lose by fifteen to twenty votes. Faced with this situation, Harding now reconsidered and, on June 20, indicated to Mondell that he would accept a temporary postponement but only to allow time for the House leadership to scrape up the necessary support.[37]

According to plan, the House recessed for six weeks on June 30, 1922, to await final Senate action on the Fordney-McCumber tariff and to "carry the subsidy bill to the people." However, subsidy proponents were unable to find an antidote for the misleading information and emotional oratory on the subsidy issue that by now were flooding many areas of the nation, especially rural southern and western communities. In the end, it was this rural sentiment that kept ship-subsidy advocates at bay, and when the House reconvened on August 15, Republican members were more than ever convinced that the administration ought to drop the proposal. Mondell and other House leaders again begged Harding to postpone the subsidy question, since there was no point in heightening party tensions so close to elections. After pondering the bill's chances, Harding reluctantly agreed and, on August 21, sent Mondell a letter accepting another postponement "until we can rivet the attention of Congress on the ship subsidy matter alone." [38] For the moment, Harding was willing to wait, but only in order to fight again another day.

If the ship-subsidy conflict presaged something more than a momentary change in the relationship between the executive and Congress, the bonus question proved that by late 1922 the two had arrived at a serious impasse in domestic affairs. Since the opening of the special session in April 1921, Congress had

37. Mondell to WGH, June 12, 1922, HP, Box 147, folder 99–4, item 71865; WGH to Mondell, June 14, 1922, HP, Box 147, folder 99–4, item 71867; WGH to Mondell, June 20, 1922, HP, Box 700, folder 10, items 152200–204.

38. WGH to Mondell, August 23, 1922, HP, Box 700, folder 10, items 152205–6.

shown a tendency to drift or erratically to go its own way. Only by practicing patience, compromise, and moderation, characteristics in keeping with Harding's personal beliefs, had the administration been able to get what it wanted. Only once before the ship-subsidy situation had the President found it necessary to intervene directly in legislative affairs (i.e., the bonus scare of midsummer 1921), and never had he tried to force an issue through Congress or crush his political opposition. Now, however, toward the end of the second session, with compromise and conciliation failing and with internal party dissension rising, Harding attempted to establish some mastery over Congress. In the case of ship subsidies he failed. In the case of the soldiers' bonus he would succeed, but at frightful cost to his party and to himself.

Revived immediately upon the opening of the second session, in December 1921, the postponed soldiers' bonus again elicited enthusiastic congressional response. Again, supported by Mellon, Harding made it known that no bonus would be acceptable unless Congress also provided funding for it. Again, congressmen quickly indicated that they intended to pass some kind of bonus despite White House objections. Obviously, passing a bonus had a personal urgency for many congressmen. They wanted to capture the serviceman's vote in the upcoming congressional elections. For that reason, Republican congressmen begged the President to accept deficit financing of a bonus if necessary, warning that the Democrats would make political capital out of either new taxes or a failure to pass a bonus. As Representative Towner (Iowa) wrote to the President in mid-February: "I earnestly hope you can see your way clear to approve a bond issue to meet the bonus demands. . . . Many members talk to me each day about the effect [a rejection] will have upon their chances of being returned. Matters are so unsettled that each new embarrassment increases their apprehension." [39]

Despite such pleas, Harding remained adamant about deficit

39. Towner to WGH, February 13, 1922, HP, Box 142, folder 95–8, item 69736.

financing and temporarily stalled bonus action. However, in direct defiance of the administration, in late March the House passed a bonus bill containing no funding provisions by the overwhelming vote of 333 to 70. After its arrival at the Senate, this House bill was given to the Finance Committee, whose chairman, Senator McCumber, was a strong bonus champion. Under his direction, the House measure was reworked, but again no funding provision was attached. Nevertheless, on May 6, McCumber rushed a copy of the Senate version to Harding with a covering letter soliciting his support. He also called on the President in person and pointed out that thirty-four senators and the entire House membership would shortly be campaigning for reelection. If the bonus was not passed, McCumber warned, the opposition of former servicemen might be fatal.[40]

Harding held firm. He recognized the political dangers involved but claimed that the stability of the nation and the need to restore prosperity came first. Like Cleveland, who was much better known for his courage, Harding seemed prepared to crucify his party on the cross of fiscal integrity if necessary. Also like Cleveland, Harding was convinced that the more responsible segments of public opinion shared his views. Such presidential obduracy caused momentary confusion in Republican senatorial ranks, and although the revised bonus bill was introduced on the floor in early June, it was not called up for debate until late August.

The fireworks started almost immediately. Debates on how to raise the more than $4 billion necessary to finance the bonus were exceptionally bitter and wholly unproductive. Democratic senators such as McKellar, Heflin, Harrison, and Thomas E. Watson reveled in the Republican confusion and claimed that GOP members were "turning their backs" on those boys who had been "in 'no man's land'" where death was raining all around." Administration supporters, on the other hand, pointed out that the home states of some of the most ardent bonus advocates (e.g., McKellar's Tennessee, Harrison's Mississippi,

40. McCumber to WGH, May 6, 1922, HP, Box 143, folder 95-10, items 69945–46.

Heflin's Alabama, and Watson's Georgia) had refused to grant
state bonuses to their veterans, while many Republican-con-
trolled northern states had already done so. They charged that
such bonus advocates were willing to gamble with the federal
treasury but not with their own state treasuries. New York's
Wadsworth, whose state had recently adopted a $40 million
bonus for its veterans, teasingly asked Heflin, whose state had
not given its veterans a dime: "Where was Alabama when that
was being done?" To the delight of his southern Democratic
colleagues, Heflin retorted: "Being robbed by New York!" [41]

On the last day of August, the Senate passed its version
of the bonus, 47 to 22, and sent it to conference. There the
House and Senate measures were quickly adjusted, and on
September 14 the House whooped the resultant product through
in twenty-five minutes. The next day, the Senate adopted it
by a vote of 36 to 17. Many senators were either absent or
were afraid to record a vote. As finally passed, the bonus bill
allowed each honorably discharged veteran to receive a service
certificate with a value of $1 per day for home service and $1.25
per day for overseas service, which, if held for twenty years,
would increase in value about three times through compound
interest. The largest paid-up amount in 1942 would be about
$1,875.

Attention now shifted to the President. In view of the high
political stakes involved, would he actually veto it? The suspense
was soon over. On September 19, Harding sent the bill back to
Congress with a message in which he expressed sympathy with
the purpose of the bonus proposal. But, he added, to increase
the public debt by one-sixth

for a distribution among less than 5,000,000 out of 110,000,000,
whether inspired by grateful sentiment or political expediency,
would undermine the confidence on which our credit is builded and
establish the precedent of distributing public funds whenever the

41. For sample debates, see *Congressional Record*, 67th Congress,
2nd Session, 8907–12, 9028–30, 9010–12, 11847–52, 11959–65, 12444–
531, 13000–13004.

proposal and the numbers affected make it seem politically appealing to do so.[42]

Both houses reacted swiftly. On September 20, just two days before the second session adjourned for the fall congressional elections, the House voted 258 to 54 to override the President's veto—forty-nine more than was necessary. The Senate vote that same afternoon was 44 to 28, four short of the required two-thirds. Seven Democrats were among the twenty-eight who upheld the President, making it a bipartisan group of such strange bedfellows as Reed Smoot, an Old Guard Republican from Utah, and Underwood, a Wilson Democrat from Alabama. It is significant, however, that not only the farm bloc but virtually every leader of his own party opposed the President on the final vote; in the House the effort to defeat him was led by Floor Leader Mondell and in the Senate by Majority Leader Lodge. Of the Republican members of the House, 188 voted to override and only 35 to sustain. In the Senate, 27 Republicans cast ballots against the President, while only 21 gave him their support. Ironically, one of the four votes Harding needed to sustain his veto was supplied by Senator Borah, who, although up for reelection, refused "to buy office out of the public treasury." [43]

Harding's veto received both praise and condemnation. In general, the business and financial community supported it, while disappointed groups like the American Legion vowed revenge at the polls. But whatever the public reaction, this bonus struggle had an important formative effect on the future relationship of the executive and Congress and on the attitudes they held toward each other. Since almost all congressional factions had expected Harding to be weak, they responded to his growing firmness with surprise, and even astonishment. Many

42. *Soldiers' Adjusted Compensation Message of the President of the United States,* 67th Congress, 2nd Session, House Document 396 (Washington, D.C., 1922).

43. New York *Times,* April 23, 1922, p. 1, quoting Borah. For final votes on the bonus, see *Congressional Record,* 67th Congress, 2nd Session, 12999–13000, 13004.

also evidenced mounting anger and alarm. Citing the bonus
veto and the presidentially sponsored drive for ship subsidies
as representing unconscionable executive intervention in congressional affairs, the Democrats, particularly southern Democrats, charged the administration with autocratic tendencies
surpassing those of Wilson. Actually, many of these Democratic
leaders were currently vacillating between condemning the administration for its "do-nothing" attitudes and charging it with
acting too vigorously. Obviously, Democratic leaders hoped to
embarrass the Republicans in any way they could and were
busily exploiting any issue that seemed to possess public appeal.
Yet the Democrats had no substitute to offer for the normalcy
program as a whole; the party's leadership consisted largely of
southerners like Garner, who had only a regional following,
and no northern or western leader had yet emerged from the
Wilson debacle to provide unity or direction. At the moment,
many congressional Democrats were less worried about the
specific aspects of the normalcy program than about the attempt
at White House mastery over Congress signified by the ship-
subsidy struggle and the soldiers'-bonus veto.

Concurrently, the farm bloc and liberal Republicans of the
LaFollette persuasion also deplored what they regarded as excessive executive interference in both these instances, declar-
ing that the President was "usurping the power of the people"
and acting in behalf of "insidious interests." Claiming that Mellon was Harding's Svengali, these individuals maintained that
the presidency was now merely the means whereby the country
was dominated by corporations and governed for the benefit of
businessmen. Even some administration supporters were a little
uneasy in the face of Harding's growing assertiveness. Their
uneasiness centered mainly on the effect such aggressiveness
might have at this particular time on Republican chances at
the polls. But underneath there was also a basic anxiety, shared
by virtually all congressional elements, that such presidential
firmness presaged a diminished role for Congress.

It is interesting that where some of the most vociferous of
the anti-administration groups had supported an aggressive ex-

ecutive during the Progressive Era, now they inveighed against it. Progressive elements, especially, no longer perceived that their best interests lay with a strong executive, at least one with Harding's political and economic beliefs. Instead, they were now espousing stronger congressional authority, believing that in that way they could best further the progressive cause. They saw in Warren Harding and his "best minds" executive system an emerging conservative dominance they did not wish to encourage or accept. Conversely, the Old Guard, many of whom had fought against the exercise of presidential power, especially as used by Theodore Roosevelt and Wilson, cheered Harding's performance in the case of ship subsidies and in the bonus fight. Their firm support of the administration in these two instances made it appear that Harding was more beholden to the Old Guard in general, and to the eastern money establishment in particular, than he actually was. Appearances to the contrary, throughout the early years of normalcy the Old Guard always remained somewhat skeptical of Harding and found his behavior either too neutral or too independent to elicit their complete support.

Harding, in turn, emerged from the battles of the second session, and especially from the bonus fight, with much greater confidence and with a more positive attitude than most of his Republican colleagues. Although he sympathized with the apprehensions of Republican congressmen, he, better than they, recognized the complex circumstances the administration faced in the late summer months of 1922. The normalcy program, which he had hoped his cabinet and Republican congressional leaders would help construct and enact, was being placed in jeopardy by the Republican party's own internal anarchy and by considerations of political expediency. He believed that the normalcy goals of tax reduction and economy in government were severely endangered by congressional demands for a soldiers' bonus, and that business recovery was being delayed by congressional refusals to adopt ship subsidies. On the one hand, he found it almost incomprehensible that he should have to fight his own party to secure these beneficial results. On the other hand, he perceived that it was his duty as president to resist economic and political folly and protect administration goals. By late 1922, therefore, Harding the congressional conciliator was clearly giving way to Harding the program protector. This was an unanticipated role for him and, as a result, he was forced to alter many of his earlier ideas about the functions of the presidency. By late 1922, the responsibilities of power and the demands of the presidential office were definitely molding Harding more than he was molding them.

Still, he might have reverted to his penchant for compromise and dodged some of the presidency's more unpleasant political burdens if he had really wanted to. He was sorely tempted. He knew, for example, that by giving in on the bonus issue alone, he could go a long way toward shoring up his deteriorating relations with Congress, woo dissident Republicans back to the fold, and eliminate an embarrassing issue from the fall elections. Some of his oldest Senate friends and congressional advisers, as well as a clear majority of his party, wanted him to do precisely that. By his own criterion of consultative consensus, he had every reason to avert a bonus showdown. But he could not bring himself to do it. As he wrote to Charles Dawes a week after the veto: "I am very sure to be very much complained against for many months to come. . . . However, I can stand that without annoyance in view of the fact that I have the satisfaction of knowing I did the wise and best thing." [44]

Few Republicans who now had to face the voters at the polls agreed with him.

44. WGH to Dawes, September 26, 1922, HP, Box 127, folder 79–5, item 62739.

4

Public Reaction
and White House
Countermoves

RARELY had a party gone into an election more confused and disunited than the Republican party in the fall of 1922. The record on which that party had to run was by no means a failure. Indeed, the record conformed remarkably to the party's campaign promises of 1920. Taxes had been lowered. A budget system had been created. A program of government savings had been effected. Numerous farm-relief measures had been enacted. Immigration had been restricted. A permanent tariff law had been passed. Relationships with former enemy states had been normalized. And a successful international disarmament conference had been held and all treaties pertaining thereto had been ratified.[1]

This record, however, had been compiled at considerable cost. The controversial nature of some of the problems, especially taxes and the tariff, had made both inter- and intra-party friction inevitable. Representing the ultimate in compromise politics, the solutions to these problems had also antagonized various political elements. Apart from southern Democrats, the most vociferous opposition had come from within the Repub-

1. In addition to the above, a Highway Act was signed into law on November 9, 1921, and a maternity bill (Sheppard-Towner) became law on November 23, 1921. Both helped fulfill campaign promises made in 1920.

lican party itself—from the farm bloc. As we have observed, this antagonism arose not so much from a clash in party principles as from the conflicting demands of postwar regional and occupational self-interest. Since 1919, such demands had subjected not only Republican politics but *all* politics to great tension and had made all issues more resistant to solution.

If Republican farm-bloc congressmen were responsible for much of the division by late 1922, the executive branch was not altogether blameless. The administration's poor judgment in encouraging the passage of the Fordney-McCumber tariff, Harding's obduracy on the bonus question and on ship subsidies, and his reluctance to exercise sustained presidential leadership combined to make matters more difficult. Moreover, the administration was vulnerable on a number of other points as well. Chief among them were Newberryism, Daugherty's various activities, and the administration's relationship with organized labor.

Attorney General Daugherty represented a continuing source of anti-administration sentiment. Caring little for popular acclaim and rough in personality, Daugherty persisted in making enemies and apparently enjoyed doing so. Such actions naturally had an adverse effect on the image of the administration as a whole. The Attorney General's failure to pursue certain war-fraud cases and his frank commitment to the spoils system antagonized not only Democrats and political liberals but even moderate elements in his own party. Consequently, most Republicans by late 1922 were convinced that Daugherty was a heavy burden for the administration to carry.

The most intense anti-Daugherty animosity came from organized labor, mainly because of his role in securing the famous Wilkerson injunction. During its first two years, the administration had tried consistently to maintain a sympathetic relationship with labor by sponsoring an unemployment conference and by mounting an assault on the twelve-hour day in the steel industry. Moreover, during the rail and coal strikes of July and August 1922, Harding had personally constructed several compromise solutions, had remained meticulously impartial, and had tried on numerous occasions to bring the contending factions together. But then, in late August, after Congress had refused to deal with the strike problem legislatively and rising public clamor demanded some kind of government intervention, Harding finally turned to the legal process and permitted Daugherty to seek from Judge James H. Wilkerson a restraining order against the rail strikers. It was believed that this injunction not only indicated Daugherty's reactionary anti-labor sentiments but symbolized the attitude toward labor of the entire administration.

It mattered little that the sweeping nature of the order was solely Daugherty's idea, that he was subsequently chastised by Harding for its punitive aspects, or that he was ordered by Harding to modify its contents. It was enough that the President had allowed him to obtain it in the first place. By causing the rail strike to be "settled" in this manner (the coal strike thereafter terminated of its own accord), Harding simultaneously obscured his own benign attitude toward workers and brought down upon his administration the hatred of organized labor. His compromising spirit and his middle-of-the-road views were obliterated by this one action, which was at variance with his usual behavior.[2]

If labor problems and Daugherty's reputation plagued the administration before the 1922 elections, they were more than matched by the issue of Newberryism. More than any other incident, Newberryism accented the chaotic, emotionally charged, and to some extent irrational political situation facing the administration by late 1922. Republican Senator Truman H. Newberry, a member of the Old Guard, had become an extremely controversial figure because a huge sum of money (over $200,000) had been expended on his behalf to defeat the automobile magnate Henry Ford for the Republican nomination for the Senate in the Michigan primary in 1918. After going on to win in the regular election in the fall, Newberry and 133 of his friends were indicted and convicted in Grand Rapids on charges of fraud, corruption, and conspiracy in con-

2. For a description of the Harding administration and organized labor, see Murray, *The Harding Era,* 227–64.

nection with his primary victory. However, neither Newberry
nor any of his friends paid a fine or went to jail, since the United
States Supreme Court reversed the decision on an appeal in
1921.

Newberry's acceptance by the Senate, meanwhile, remained
in doubt, as angry disagreement concerning his fate intermit-
tently erupted in that body for over two years. Senators who
advocated his exclusion coined the word "Newberryism" as a
synonym for buying public office. Farm-bloc senators such as
LaFollette and Norris eagerly seized upon this case as an example of the "money power" in American politics and persistently used it as a weapon in their struggles with business interests in their own party. Democratic senators appropriated
the issue as the basis for some emotional oratory and for bitter
assaults on Republican policies in general. Senator Underwood,
for example, once claimed that "it is not Senator Truman H.
Newberry who is under indictment in this case; it is the Republican Party." [3] Senator Heflin saw "the slimy trail of the
boodle serpent" extending in all directions from the Michigan
Senator, while Caraway and McKellar gloomily predicted that
his admisson would cause the American Senate to follow the
Roman Senate "into ruin and oblivion." [4]

Both as senator and as president, Harding had supported
Newberry's right to his seat. Because of this attitude, Newberryism automatically became an important anti-administration issue. Thus, the final Senate vote on Newberry on January 12,
1922, involved the prestige of the administration as much as
the reputation of one man. At that time, forty-six senators upheld Newberry's claim to his seat, while forty-one voted to
exclude him. This vote reflected not only the Senate's judgment on Newberry's qualifications but also the current division
in that body over administration policies. Immediately after
the victory, Harding sent Newberry a congratulatory letter,

3. *Congressional Record,* 67th Congress, 2nd Session, 1051.
4. See sample debates on Newberry in *Congressional Record,* 67th
Congress, 1st Session, 7682–97, 7789–94, 7806–8, 8040–48; 67th Congress, 2nd Session, 830–32, 989–99.

saying, "I am greatly pleased at the outcome," [5] Widely broad-
cast, this letter was used thereafter by anti-administration
forces to prevent the Newberry case from being forgotten, and
by the time of the November elections, charges of Newberryism, especially in the agrarian West, evoked the image not
only of a tarnished personal reputation but of an administration that had defiled itself by supporting him.

In view of this background, it is little wonder that congressional Republicans faced the fall elections with apprehension.
By emphasizing the weaknesses of the executive, many of them
hoped to shift blame for their party's plight solely onto the President-
dent. As a result, the administration was subjected to heavy
pounding from virtually every quarter. Curiously, despite the
President's obvious shortcomings, public acceptance of the activities of the executive branch (except for Daugherty) remained strong throughout 1921–22, while popular acceptance of
Congress was never more than lukewarm.[6] Still, Harding was
enough of a realist to know that the fate of his administration
was bound together with that of all Republicans regardless of
their specific views or what the popularity polls showed. If Republican congressmen were to be beaten, it would be seen as a
defeat for the normalcy program as well. Harding also realized
that the farm-bloc schism made some losses inevitable. Shortly
before the election, he confided to Malcolm Jennings that for
this and other reasons, the party was probably no more than
25 percent as strong as it had been in 1920. But the main factor
in this decline, Harding thought, was the country's failure to
experience a return to prosperity. The various remedies that
had been adopted had not yet had time to work. As he wrote
to an Ohio friend, Daniel R. Crissinger, "A lot of people have
persuaded themselves that the distressing agricultural situation

5. WGH to Newberry, January 12, 1922, HP, Box 701, folder 8,
item 152573.

6. Long before the election, the New York *Times* put it this way:
"Congressmen would be well pleased to have the country look at the
President instead of too hard at themselves." New York *Times*, March
4, 1922, p. 14. See also Mark Sullivan, "National Politics in 1922,"
World's Work, XLIII, No. 4 (February 1922), 361–62.

and the widespread unemployment is chargeable to this administration. I do not know how we can correct this impression until time has joined in the argument." [7]

Time had run out for many Republican congressmen by the fall of 1922. The primaries in the spring and summer had already foreshadowed the trend. In Indiana, Senator Harry S. New, a close friend of Harding who had voted for Newberry and against the bonus, was defeated for the Republican nomination by former Senator Albert J. Beveridge. In the Pennsylvania primary, Gifford Pinchot, a liberal Republican with anti-administration feelings, won the gubenatorial nomination over a regular machine-backed Republican. In Iowa, Smith W. Brookhart, an outspoken critic of the administration, was nominated to the senatorial vacancy created by Senator Kenyon's elevation to the federal bench. In Wisconsin, Senator LaFollette won renomination easily. But of all the primary results, none was more shocking than the defeat of Senator McCumber of North Dakota at the hands of the politically inept Lynn J. Frazier. McCumber was a Senate veteran of almost twenty-five years and was regarded as an administration stalwart even though he had deserted the President on the bonus. Contemporary pundits could only explain this upset by McCumber's association with the tariff and his support of Newberry.

This general pattern was repeated on election day, November 7. In Indiana, Beveridge, having beaten New in the primary, lost to former Governor Samuel M. Ralston, a Democrat. In New Jersey, Senator Frelinghuysen, one of Harding's old friends, lost to former Democratic governor Edward I. Edwards. In Michigan, Representative Fordney, a member of Congress since 1899, lost his seat. In Wisconsin, Senator LaFollette won a thumping majority. In Minnesota, Senator Kellogg was beaten by an anti-administration candidate, Farmer-Laborite Henrik Shipstead. In Iowa, Brookhart won and added another rural radical member to the Senate. In all, the Republicans lost seven Senate seats while the Democrats picked up six, not in-

7. WGH to Crissinger, January 19, 1922, HP, Box 47, folder 21–8, item 22250.

cluding Farmer-Laborite Shipstead, thus cutting the Republican majority from twenty-four to ten. In the House, the Republicans lost seventy seats and the Democrats gained seventy-six, reducing the Republican majority to twenty-six and placing the balance of power squarely in the hands of maverick Republicans and the farm bloc.

The reasons for this setback were the subject of much speculation. Secretary Hoover believed that the chief cause was the machinations of the farm bloc. Secretary Wallace thought that it resulted from a simple lack of understanding of administration goals in the rural areas. Other administration supporters claimed that general congressional divisiveness and a vacillating congressional leadership had been responsible. On the other hand, anti-administration observers said it was the executive's fault and pointed to Newberryism and the Wilkerson injunction. Most press discussions centered on the tariff and the bonus. As for his own assessment of the election, Harding isolated two factors: 1) farmer discontent and 2) labor opposition. Otherwise he could see no pattern to the outcome.[8]

The election did result in severe Republican losses, a majority of them being administration supporters. But it was not the debacle that some observers made it out to be. The incumbent party still had control of both houses, unlike the situation under Arthur in 1882, Harrison in 1890, Cleveland in 1894, Taft in 1910, or Wilson in 1918. Moreover, the election had provided no genuine trial of strength on clearly definable issues. Much depended on local conditions, and there seemed to be no unity among the opposition except a vague general discontent. In some areas, even anti-administration Republicans were turned out of office for no apparent reason by Democratic opponents who had nothing in particular to offer. Despite widespread claims to the contrary, the election was not a public repudiation of the normalcy program.

Regardless of the precise reasons for the reversal or what it showed, one thing was clear—the relationship between the

8. WGH to Reily, November 22, 1922, HP, Box 362, folder 2571-1, item 171808, containing a synopsis of Harding's views.

executive and Congress needed immediate attention or a further deterioration in Republican prospects was likely. Up to this moment, Harding had taken two different and contradictory approaches to Congress—one conciliatory and the other uncompromising. Neither had provided the necessary party *esprit* or given Republicans in Congress a sense of unity. Not surprisingly, Republican congressmen were divided over a remedy. Some pro-administration House members claimed that what was needed was stronger presidential guidance, and warned that unless the White House provided it, congressional and party anarchy would continue to grow. Somewhat less eagerly, administration supporters in the Senate also voiced this view. But Republican farm-bloc senators did not, nor did insurgent Republican House members. Moreover, the suspicion lingers that although numerous pro-administration congressmen grumbled about the "lack of executive direction," they too really preferred a presidential "hands-off" policy. In those instances when Harding had shown real presidential firmness, more of them had been antagonized than pleased. Despite what they said, almost all Republican congressmen apparently believed that for the moment the wisest course was for both the President and Congress to mark time until adjournment in March 1923, the President reverting to non-involvement and Congress passing only the necessary housekeeping legislation.

With the election of 1922, Harding's transformation as chief protector and sponsor of the normalcy program was almost complete. Whatever hopes he had for a revitalized and reunified congressional leadership totally disappeared. That leadership had already suffered badly from attrition. Senator Knox had died in October 1921, and Senator Penrose on the last day of that year. Senator Lodge's influence had waned drastically. Now the election defeats of McCumber and Kellogg were additionally debilitating. In the House, the continued vacillation of such leaders as Gillett, Edmonds, and Campbell, as well as the election loss of Fordney and Mondell, foreshadowed further difficulty. If a revitalized leadership was to be provided, it would have to come from the White House. Moreover, it was obvious that, in view of the election, the new 68th Congress would be even less tractable and less responsive to presidential pressure than the present one. Therefore, it seemed to Harding that whatever he hoped to accomplish in relation to the normalcy program had better be pushed for before March 4. Fortunately, all but one of the major parts of that program had already been passed. That one—ship subsidies—still remained.

The ship-subsidy issue now served as the vehicle by which Harding finally emerged as a practitioner of strong presidential power, deserting most of his former beliefs concerning presidential proprieties. As early as October 16, three weeks before the election, Harding had written to a congressman friend that he was inclined, no matter what the election showed, to call a special session of Congress "not later than November 20th, in order to get this exceedingly important legislation underway." [9] On November 9, just two days after the election, Harding issued a call for an extra session to begin on November 20 and bluntly warned Congress that he would settle for nothing less than passage of the postponed ship-subsidy bill.

Harding could hardly have selected a worse time or a more unsuitable topic on which to conduct a decisive test of will with Congress. His call for the passage of ship subsidies reintroduced a most controversial issue and further aggravated the existing divisions in the Republican party. It also opened the administration to charges of using a discredited lame-duck congress to ram through administration-sponsored legislation. By this action, Harding was consciously turning back the congressional-executive relationship to that of the late Wilson era, but this time the acrimony revolved around domestic affairs. Understandably, deep gloom pervaded most pro-administration members when Congress reconvened in extra session on November 20.

Even before the roll was called, anti-administration forces drew blood. Facing another challenge to his seat and not wishing to suffer further personal insults, Senator Newberry suddenly

9. WGH to B. L. Rosenbloom, October 16, 1922, HP, Box 148, folder 99–7, item 72124.

announced his resignation. Two days later, Harding himself stepped onto the congressional battlefield, armed like the partisan gladiator he claimed he would never be, and delivered a hard-hitting address. Applauded only three times during his speech, he attacked the opposition to ship subsidies, condemned geographic and economic partisanship, and pointedly told his agrarian opponents: "Frankly I think it loftier statesmanship to support and commend a policy designed to effect the larger good of the nation than merely to record the too-hasty expressions of a constituency." [10]

Such presidential lecturing and bluntness did little to smooth over differences between the administration and its enemies, but it did serve as a warning that the White House was preparing to play rough. As debate on the subsidy bill got under way in the House, the President maintained a check on the attitudes of all Republican members and leaked word that those who did not support the administration could expect no further consideration in patronage matters. For the first time in his tenure, Harding began to screen his congressional callers, indicating that those who opposed him on ship subsidies were no longer welcome at the White House. He notified Gillett, Towner, and Mondell that he expected the House leadership to reduce defections on this issue to an absolute minimum. Simultaneously, he ordered his cabinet to apply pressure in whatever way they could on behalf of ship subsidies. More significant, he cautioned Secretary Wallace, who remained lukewarm on the subsidy issue, against dragging his feet, and directed him to win over as many agrarian leaders as he could. Obviously, Harding was beginning to use his "best minds" executive system in a somewhat different manner than he had originally intended and to apply to Congress some of those harsh presidential pressures which, as a senator, he had so deplored. The results were temporarily gratifying. Despite frenzied Democratic opposition, the White House whip finally produced a majority, and on November 29, when the

10. Harding, *Speeches as President,* "Message of the President of the United States to Congress, November 21, 1922," 5.

final House roll call was taken, the vote was 208 to 184, a margin of twenty-four.[11]

The day the subsidy bill passed, Harding wrote a friend: "We [will] have a more difficult contest in the Senate than we had in the House, because of the lack of limitation on debate and the inability to restrict debaters to the pending question." [12] He was correct. Also complicating the situation in the Senate was the fact that its consideration of ship subsidies necessarily extended beyond December 4, the date when the extra (actually, the third) session automatically expired and, by law, the second regular (fourth) session of the 67th Congress began. As a result, the ship-subsidy bill became entangled with other important measures in the waning months before the March 4 adjournment.

Unhappily, the most significant piece of legislation adversely affected by this entanglement was the so-called Dyer anti-lynching bill, which would have made lynching a "national" crime subject to federal prosecution and penalty. Harding had requested such legislation in his first message to Congress in April 1921, and the Negro community had strongly supported it. Passed by the House in January 1922, the Dyer bill languished thereafter in the Senate Judiciary Committee because of southern opposition. However, with the opening of the extra session on November 20, the bill finally reached the Senate floor. Thus, while the House was discussing the ship-subsidy measure, the Senate became embroiled in bitter debate over the anti-lynching proposal.

At the same time the House passed the subsidy bill, a Democratic minority from the Border states and the former Confederacy began a filibuster in the Senate against the Dyer measure. For a week these southern leaders talked on, blocking consideration of all other legislation, including the House-passed sub-

11. *Congressional Record,* 67th Congress, 3rd Session, 429, final House vote.
12. WGH to J. T. Williams, Jr., November 29, 1922, HP, Box 704, folder 7, item 168677.

sidy bill. Realizing the futility of continuing the impasse longer,
the Republican caucus voted on December 2 to drop the Dyer
proposal in order to clear the way for Senate consideration of
the subsidy matter. As Lodge explained to the press: "Of course,
the Republicans feel very strongly, as I do, that the bill ought to
become law [but] we had to choose between giving up the
whole session to a protracted filibuster or going ahead with the
regular business of the session." [13]

It was unfair for the black community to blame the administration for the defeat of the Dyer bill, as it subsequently did.
But it was certainly true that the abandonment of this measure
was hastened by the administration's desire for ship subsidies.
As it turned out, it made no difference. The strategy of the opponents of ship subsidies was precisely the same as for the Dyer
bill. That struggle actually provided them with a dress rehearsal.
First, an attempt was made by skillful parliamentary maneuver-
ing to force a displacement of the subsidy proposal on the Senate calendar by other bills. When that failed, a filibuster was
organized.

Leading the opposition against subsidies was the same phal-
anx of Border-state and southern senators who had killed the
Dyer bill. But now they were joined by midwestern and western senators who shortly before had morally condemned these
Southerners for using filibuster methods. Conducting the fight
for subsidies was a curious coalition drawn from East, West, and
some Gulf Coast states. Party lines were sundered by these
geographic groupings, indicating the degree to which party discipline had declined by early 1923. Both sides in the conflict in-
dulged in calumny and name-calling, but anti-subsidy men were
particularly emotional. Republicans in this group kept widening
the already serious intra-party agrarian-business split, while
Democrats enthusiastically abetted them. "Pat" Harrison, for
example, derided the Republican leadership for pushing ship
subsidies while important farm legislation again lay on the table. Harrison was referring to a new plan recently proposed by
Norris for a program of farm subsidies. Harrison's real motive

13. New York *Times*, December 3, 1922, p. 1, quoting Lodge.

in mentioning this matter later became obvious when he voted against the Norris plan himself. Meanwhile, LaFollette, who backed virtually any kind of subsidy aid to farmers, made bombastic speeches denouncing the indefensibility, unconstitutionality, and callousness of subsidies for the shipping industry.[14]

By the end of January 1923, it was clear that the opposition's tactics were succeeding. Harding's ability to force recalcitrant senators into line, especially farm-bloc senators, proved to be much less successful than with House members, and in desperation the administration tried one last ploy. On February 7, Harding appeared before both houses of Congress, ostensibly to inform them of the results of current World War I debt-funding negotiations between the United States and Great Britain. But a significant part of his speech was directed at the Senate and was devoted to ship subsidies. "I plead for a decision," he said, and demanded that the bill not be killed by further delaying tactics.[15]

The Senate would not listen. On February 19, a filibuster began when Senator Morris Sheppard of Texas talked for ten hours. Other volunteers quickly took over—LaFollette, Reed, Borah. Senator McKellar, one of the filibuster's star performers, claimed that the November elections had already shown that the public wanted nothing to do with this measure. The majority of the Republican party did not want the bill either, said McKellar, "but they do not want to fall out with the Executive. They do not want to come to the parting of the ways with him." [16]

A parting of the ways was at hand. On Friday, February 23, as the ship-subsidy filibuster entered its fifth day, Senator Charles Curtis, acting floor leader, called on the President and laid the facts before him. The situation was critical. The filibuster was creating an embarrassing log jam and was preventing the final passage of certain needed appropriations. Even though it seemed hopeless, the White House asked Curtis to try

14. For sample opinion, see *Congressional Record,* 67th Congress, 4th Session, 508–21, 746.
15. Harding's speech in *ibid.,* 3212–14.
16. *Ibid.,* 4227, 4230, quoting McKellar.

once more to break the filibuster over the weekend. However, on Saturday afternoon, when Senator Jones of Washington, a strong subsidy advocate, turned up in the Senate sporting a white tie in place of the red one he had been wearing, Senator Harrison asked him if the change signified surrender. Amid much laughter, Jones replied, "Certainly, I recognize when I am beaten." [17] Shortly thereafter, pro-administration senators voted to drop the subsidy bill in favor of other legislation.

The remaining few days of the 67th Congress were anti-climactic. Several appropriation bills were passed, an administration-sponsored Government Reclassification Act for federal employees was endorsed, and another Wallace-initiated and farm-bloc-supported rural-credits act (Agricultural Intermediate Credits Act of 1923) was added to those many farm-relief measures already enacted. Besides the ship-subsidy matter, the only item of business left hanging was a last-minute presidential proposal for American membership on the World Court. Submitted to the Senate on February 24, 1923, this request was immediately given to the Senate Foreign Relations Committee, where a surprised Senator Lodge stalled for time.

The March 4 adjournment of the 67th Congress was a welcome relief for everyone. Even though that Congress had not treated the administration as badly as the frequent tension between the White House and Capitol Hill suggested, the appearance was more obvious than the substance, and both the executive and the lawmakers were delighted to terminate their relationship. Having suffered through four separate sessions and having been addressed by the President no less than six times, congressmen were understandably happy to shake the dust of Washington from their feet. But as the *New Republic* said, "The American citizen to whom the passing of the old Congress is a source of the most unalloyed satisfaction is President Harding." [18] Indeed, Harding longed for a respite from the mounting warfare between himself and Congress, and he was weary of the

17. *Ibid.*, 4470.
18. "The Dilemma of the Party Politicians," *New Republic* XXXIV, No. 433 (March 21, 1923), 82.

factionalism, regional selfishness, and self-righteous pomposity that many of the congressional debates had revealed. While most congressmen returned home, Harding took a brief golfing holiday in Florida both to forget the cares of his office and to dispel the lingering effects of a severe attack of the flu, which had struck him in mid-January. However, American politics knows no vacation, and although the President was still not fully rested, he returned to Washington in April to consult with party leaders and plan strategy for the months ahead.

In the spring of 1923, Republicans were far more worried about their party's image than about the President's health. Many felt that there was too much misunderstanding about normalcy goals and that a broad program of public education had to be initiated. Party leaders in particular believed that, in view of the 1922 elections, "heroic" measures were now required to make the nation appreciate what had been accomplished. It is significant that they turned to Harding to rectify the situation. Even some of the President's erstwhile congressional opponents now looked to the White House. Despite his sharp differences with Congress—indeed, perhaps because of them—Harding by 1923 had clearly emerged as the most important leader in his party. Already serving as the chief catalyst in the functioning of the executive branch, he was becoming the most critical factor in the legislative process as well. Although party insurgents had successfully blocked one of his most cherished proposals—ship subsidies—all Republican congressmen could see that other executive-congressional battles lay ahead unless the President got his way, and that he intended to dominate the political situation.

A truly significant change had taken place in the White House. Harding no longer gave evidence of being merely a conciliator, or even a program protector; he had became an initiator and partisan fighter. Now, as a result of the debacle of 1922 and the various events surrounding the closing sessions of the 67th Congress, opponents and proponents alike sensed that the Republican party's destiny rested largely on Harding's shoulders and that, tired as he was, he would have to

extend himself if momentum was to be regained and if further
Republican successes were to be achieved. As the New York
Times saw it, the President would at least have to "go before
the people" and make a "swing around the circle." Others
agreed that "Mr. Harding, and Mr. Harding alone, can furnish
the incentive for a Republican rally." [19]

As the summer months of 1923 approached, the administration stood on firm ground politically. By that time, most of the
party's campaign promises of 1920 had been fulfilled. Not all
of this fulfillment would later, with the onset of the Great Depression, prove to have been wise. But at the moment it represented a considerable political success. Moreover, the "best
minds" executive system that Harding had established seemed
to be operating excellently in contrast with the old Wilson
arrangement. The State Department under Hughes was sur-
mounting the animosities of the Wilson years and was rapidly
adjusting the nation's foreign policies to the realities of the postwar world. Secretary Hoover and the Commerce Department
were currently delighting the business community with their
efficiency and various pro-business activities. Secretary Mellon
and the Treasury Department were drastically reducing the national debt and monitoring cutbacks in federal expenditures.
Even Secretary Wallace and the Agriculture Department, farm-
bloc appearances notwithstanding, were retaining the confidence
of most agrarian leaders and considering ever more radical ways
to approach the farm problem.[20]

But of all the factors helping the administration, none was
so important as the first glow of returning prosperity. This factor
was doubly important for Harding, since at the moment there
was already speculation about the 1924 nominations. Harding
had always counted heavily on a return of prosperity to reduce
anti-administration criticism, and as the economy rapidly gained
momentum in the spring of 1923, he became increasingly opti-

19. New York *Times,* February 5, 1923, p. 6.
20. For an analysis of these departmental activities, see Murray,
The Harding Era, 129–66, 172–79, 191–98, 199–202, 327–75, 376–
416.

mistic about his own and his party's chances. He sensed that the normalcy program was gaining in public favor, and in a burst of confidence in May he wrote to an anxious Marion supporter, "There can not possibly be any doubt about renomination." [21]

It was true that even in the face of rumors concerning the possible candidacies of grumpy Hiram Johnson and ambitious Bob LaFollette, the overwhelming majority of Republican politicians were remaining with the President. Even lukewarm supporters of normalcy policies stayed in the Harding camp. The election of 1922 had forced a realization that, except for those who really wanted to leave the party, all Republicans were in the same fix. Either they would succeed with the normalcy administration or they would fall with it. Hiram Johnson finally perceived this, and by early June he disclaimed any intention of contesting the Ohioan for the nomination. By that time, even the most ardent anti-administration farm-bloc partisan could see that business growth was beginning to dissipate much of the earlier criticism. Everyone could see it, that is, except Senator LaFollette, who continued on his lonely way.

Such was the political situation when Harding left on his ill-fated trip to Alaska in mid-June 1923. The immediate purpose of the journey was to provide the President with a first-hand view of Alaska and its potential for growth and development. But the trip was also designed to allow the President to escape Washington's summer heat and to "stump the country" on behalf of the normalcy program. All along the road to Alaska, and then all the way back, he was scheduled to make speeches, advertise his personality, and engage in political haymaking. For both himself and the American people it was to be, in his own words, "a voyage to understanding." [22]

When the presidential car *Superb* left Washington on June 20, Harding was already aware of some of the scandals that would later tarnish his administration. As a result, it was after-

21. WGH to Charles C. Fisher, May 19, 1923, HP, Box 696, folder 8, item 150132.
22. The plans and procedures for the western trip are in HP, Box 151, folder 101–2.

ward claimed that he literally worried himself to death on the Alaskan trip. Undoubtedly, anxiety did fill the last several months of his life, but by the late spring of 1923 his ill health was physiological, not merely psychosomatic. Following his attack of the flu in January, he had experienced increasing difficulty in sleeping at night, and when he lay down he could not breathe. Alarmed by this, he had changed his regimen, but nothing seemed to help; his normal ruddy color turned to a pallor and fatigue stooped his frame. Shortly before the Alaska trip, a concerned Secretary Hughes confided to his wife that the President's blood pressure was consistently above 175. E. Mont Reily reported that after having dinner with him in late May, Harding had said, "I am sick—I am all in. . . . I need rest." In early June, Senator Frank B. Willis of Ohio went to the White House to discuss five items with the President but returned to his office after having discussed only two. When his secretary asked why, Willis replied, "Warren seemed so tired." [23]

The pace of the western trip would have been strenuous for a well man; for a sick man it was killing. Despite warnings from his physicians, Harding adhered to his rigorous speaking schedule as the presidential party moved westward to Tacoma, where, on July 5, he was to board the U.S.S. *Henderson* for the passage to Alaska. At first the crowds were small and not especially responsive. But as Harding moved farther west, the crowds became larger and more demonstrative. Sticking closely to his "voyage to understanding" theme, Harding delivered fourteen major addresses and innumerable whistle-stoppers in a little over two weeks, outlining his political and economic beliefs as of mid-1923. No such series of presidential speeches occurred again until the fireside chats of Franklin Roosevelt.

Surprisingly reflective, yet at the same time forward-looking, these speeches were often lost in the colorful press reporting of the drama and the excitement surrounding the presidential pilgrimage. In them, Harding announced his firm support for

23. Merlo J. Pusey, *Charles Evans Hughes* (New York, 1951), II, 562; Reily, "Years of Confusion," 449; interview by Robert K. Murray with C. A. Jones, November 2, 1966.

American membership in the World Court, thus signaling a retreat from the hard-line isolationism of the post-Wilson period. He also advocated continued remedial legislation for the farmer, but did not intimate that he was yet prepared to follow Secretary Wallace in more radical approaches to the farm problem. He warned of future crises in transportation, and prophesied that unless the railroads increased their efficiency and consolidated into a smaller number of systems, ultimate bankruptcy and government ownership would result. He expressed faith in the further development of commercial aviation, the automobile, and the radio, and proclaimed the necessity for both local and national regulation in these areas. He strongly advocated the expansion of a national integrated highway network and its joint development by the states and the federal government. He again expressed his belief that labor unions were beneficial and that workers had a right to organize and strike. But he rejected any domination of the economy by unions.

At all times, Harding reaffirmed his administration's dedication to business progress and to business-government cooperation. But he also warned that unless business remained responsive to public needs and fair to labor, the necessary reforms would be forced upon it. He confidently predicted an era of long-term prosperity and lauded the accomplishments of the normalcy program in government economy, tax decreases, and debt reduction—three achievements he believed were contributing greatly to economic recovery. With regard to conservation, Harding urged a wise and steady development of the nation's natural resources so that they would not be either recklessly exploited or subject to statutory nonuse. Specifically, he advocated cooperation between the various states and the federal government in planning in the areas of land reclamation, irrigation, and water power. Harding also urged the better conservation of human resources, and to this end suggested the creation of a carefully monitored local-federal program of Americanization. In another forward-looking move, Harding harked back to his first message to Congress in April 1921, and again recommended establishing a Department of Public Welfare to unify and coordinate all the federal government's welfare activities for the American people. Finally, he reaffirmed his belief in a strong merchant marine and said that he would not rest until he saw America supreme on the high seas.[24]

By the time Harding reached Tacoma, it was clear that in these speeches he had spoken not only as President but as the undisputed leader of the Republican party. Through these speeches he was also foreshadowing a "new" normalcy, somewhat more innovative and broader-based than the existing one. His call for a sharing of responsibility by federal and local governments in such areas as welfare and internal improvements certainly did not presage the total federal withdrawal many business conservatives desired. It was significant also, as most observers commented, how silent his agrarian opponents became as he moved westward, balancing hard-sell campaigning with grandiloquent pronouncements. The press in particular agreed that these western speeches were fashioning the Republican platform for 1924 and showed a much abler and far more statesmanlike Harding than the one the nation had overwhelmingly elected in 1920. Newspapermen covering the trip were especially struck by his confidence, his independence, and his courage. Harding seemed no longer, as in 1920, to be so dependent on consultations with party leaders, appeared to be virtually free of the influence of the Old Guard, and was eschewing those traditional appeals to political expediency that usually mar presidential addresses. The various elements in his party were now beginning to take their cue from him rather than he from them. He was no longer merely the first among equals in a collective party leadership. Increasingly, *he* was setting the guidelines, *he* was announcing the goals, *he* was outlining the plans.[25]

There is no indication that by mid-1923 Harding had consciously given up all of his former ideas concerning the role and

24. All the western addresses are published in full in Harding, *Speeches as President*.
25. "Mr. Harding Foreshadows His 1924 Platform," *Literary Digest*, LXXVIII, No. 3 (July 21, 1923), 9.

functions of the presidency. He still regarded conciliation, compromise, friendliness, and humility as superior personal and political traits. But as chief executive he was now operating in a manner different from what these beliefs would suggest. Since Harding was not the philosophical type, he did not analyze this growing paradox in any of his speeches or leave any systematic written record of his reaction to it. Only in stray comments and occasional references in letters did he indicate that he even knew a significant change in his behavior had taken place. In any event, during the closing sessions of the 67th Congress and in the intervening months before his death, his actions spoke for themselves and comprise a fascinating study in the development of executive attitudes and in the transforming quality of the presidential office.

As for the western trip, Harding arrived at Tacoma satisfied. Talking to crowds of people buoyed his spirits, and, for the moment, some of his weariness and anxiety slipped away. But the respite was only temporary. The Alaskan leg of his journey was especially tiring as he moved from one small northern community to another, and by the time the presidential party arrived back in the United States on July 27, reporters in Seattle openly remarked about the President's spent condition.[26] To suggestions that he curtail some of his activities, Harding insisted that the original schedule be followed and, hatless and in a fierce sun, delivered a major speech that very day to a large midafternoon crowd in the University of Washington stadium. The theme of his address was the "discovery of Alaska," and its high point was his prophecy that Alaska was destined for eventual statehood. It was a good speech, but he delivered it

26. "The President and the People," *Outlook,* CXXXIV, No. 12 (August 8, 1923), 535. Alaskan Notes, HHP, Box 1–I/546, provide one of the best eyewitness accounts on the Alaskan trip. Compare with Hoover, *Memoirs,* II, 48–52. Another eyewitness account is a twenty-one-page report of Ernest Chapman, a railroad policeman who accompanied the presidential party (HP, Box 765, dated September 11, 1923). These accounts eliminate many of the myths about the trip. For an examination of these myths and the inaccuracies concerning the journey, see Murray, *The Harding Era,* 439–48.

listlessly, his voice failing several times. Members of his party, among them Hoover, urged him to return at once to his private car. But it was not until later that evening that he was able to get away and go to bed.

There was nothing mysterious about subsequent events, although later writers tried to make them so. During the night, as the train moved down the West Coast toward San Francisco, the President suffered a cardiac malfunction that was not immediately diagnosed. En route the next day, Harding felt better, dressed himself, and upon his arrival in San Francisco shunned the wheel chair that had been provided for him. Despite the protests of his doctors, he walked unaided to a waiting car, which drove him to reserved rooms in the Palace Hotel, where he was again put to bed. There it was established that he had had a heart attack, and he was treated accordingly. Three days later, responding well to rest and medication, he was propped up in bed listening to Mrs. Harding read to him when the end suddenly came.[27]

The nation was stunned by the first news of the President's illness. Not even the most irascible of Harding's political enemies failed to show genuine anxiety and concern over his condition. His death immediately plunged the country into deep mourning, as all citizens reacted with an outpouring of feeling. Now it was not the rising executive-congressional tension or Harding's growing firmness that was remembered, but his kindness, his friendliness, his moderation, and his humaneness. As his funeral train left San Francisco and moved eastward, thousands upon thousands of citizens, mindful of the dead President's gentle spirit, lined the right of way, with their heads bowed in silence or humming his favorite hymns. Veteran reporters assigned to the trip were awed by the crowds; they had never seen anything like it. In Washington, similar scenes occurred, as long lines filed by his body while it lay in state in the Capitol rotunda. After funeral services were concluded there, the final trip to Marion once again witnessed saddened citizens lining the

27. For the exact circumstances surrounding his death, see *ibid.*, 448–51.

tracks along the way. In that small Ohio town, the casket was placed on a hearse, which wound slowly past the *Star* building, where the presses stood silent, and through streets down which shouting delegations had trooped on their way to his front porch in the summer of 1920. At last, at a secluded, shaded cemetery, the hearse gave up its burden. For the moment, at least, Warren Harding was what he most wanted to be: the nation's best-loved president.[28]

28. For the events between August 3 and August 11, the contemporary press is the best source. The New York *Tribune* is excellent on the train trips and the Marion funeral. The Washington *Post* is best on the activities in the capital.

5

The Rhetoric
of Corruption

LESS THAN SEVEN months after Harding was laid in his grave, Secretary of State Hughes felt constrained to conclude a eulogy to his dead chief at a joint memorial service of both houses of Congress with the following words:

> We, who look on with critics' eyes,
> Exempt from action's crucial test,
> Human ourselves, at least are wise
> In honoring one who did his best.[1]

Representing a spirited defense of the normalcy program as well as of the man who had directed it, this eulogy was specifically designed to blunt some of the rising criticism caused by the emerging public knowledge of the so-called Harding scandals. As this knowledge grew, however, no number of eulogies or appeals to sympathy would rescue either Harding's reputation or that of his administration from disgrace. In neither case, Hughes's plea to the contrary, would best ever be good enough.

Harding was still alive when the earliest indications of corruption began to filter through. The first incident came to the President's attention in the winter of 1923 and involved Charles R. Forbes, director of the Veterans' Bureau. Forbes, a World War I hero, had worked for the Republican ticket in the Northwest during the campaign of 1920. Through flattery and a flair for cards, Forbes had ingratiated himself with the President,

1. The eulogy is in *Congressional Record,* 68th Congress, 1st Session, 3318–23.

who appointed him to the Veterans' post largely on a whim. Daugherty never liked Forbes, and at the time of his appointment he warned Harding that it was a mistake. Dr. Charles E. Sawyer, Harding's personal physician, also distrusted Forbes and early suspected him of venal activities. Indeed, it was Sawyer who initially urged the President to look into Forbes's handling of his office. Harding at first refused to believe that anything was amiss, but then had to change his mind as evidence collected by both Daugherty and Dr. Sawyer began to mount.

It was soon apparent that Forbes was illegally selling government supplies and engaging in undercover deals relating to hospital building contracts and site selections. Shocked by such disclosures, Harding alternated for a time between rage and despondency. Finally, he called Forbes to the White House and demanded his resignation, but permitted him to leave the country first. A thoroughly frightened Forbes hastily booked passage for Europe and, once there, resigned on February 15, 1923.[2]

The White House sought to keep the circumstances surrounding Forbes's resignation secret. Harding was naturally fearful of the political consequences of publicly admitting Forbes's venality or of calling for congressional help in exposing his crimes. At the moment, prospects for the Republican party were brightening and the last thing the administration wanted was a government scandal. However, all White House attempts at secrecy failed as gossip about Forbes's activities began to circulate. The gossip finally reached such a point that, two weeks after his resignation, the Senate on its own initiative ordered a full-scale investigation into the operations of the Veterans' Bureau.

Forbes's resignation was but the first in a series of events in the late winter and early spring of 1923 that pointed to corrupt

2. For two colorful, but somewhat fictionalized, accounts of the Forbes-Harding confrontation, see Samuel Hopkins Adams, *Incredible Era: The Life and Times of Warren Gamaliel Harding* (Boston, 1939), 294–97, and Sullivan, *Our Times,* VI, 238–42.

activities in the administration. Within the next three months, two mysterious suicides shocked the Washington political community. On March 14, standing before his bathroom mirror, Charles F. Cramer, general counsel of the Veterans' Bureau and confident of Forbes, put a .45 caliber bullet through his right temple. Then, on the morning of May 30, Jess Smith, Attorney General Daugherty's personal secretary and Jack-of-all-trades, blew his brains out in Daugherty's Washington apartment. Although the information given to the press claimed that Cramer had killed himself because of "personal financial reverses" and that Smith was depressed because of his severe diabetes, the White House knew better. Cramer was involved with Forbes in graft regarding hospital construction sites, while Smith had been peddling influence on the strength of his close association with Daugherty. Just before Smith's death, Harding had received intimations of Smith's illegal dealings and had ordered Daugherty to "get him out of Washington." It was this presidential order rather than his diabetes that caused Smith to take his life.

How detailed Harding's knowledge was of Smith's activities is open to conjecture.[3] But it was enough to make him realize that his administration was more tainted by corruption than he had at first supposed. Actually, Smith's suicide had a particularly devastating effect on the White House. Harding immediately lost some of the optimism with which he had greeted the first signs of returning prosperity, and he began to worry—a condition that was clearly evident on his ill-fated Alaskan trip.

On October 22, 1923, not quite three months after Harding's death, the Senate investigation of the Veterans' Bureau began. In view of the recent tense relations between that body and the executive, there were those congressmen who were anxious to use the investigation as a springboard for an intensi-

3. For Harding's knowledge about Smith, see "Reminiscences of James W. Wadsworth," 279; interview by Robert K. Murray with C. A. Jones, November 2, 1966; and *Investigation of the Honorable Harry M. Daugherty,* U.S. Senate Select Committee, 68th Congress, 1st Session (Washington, D.C., 1924), I, 538–45, and *passim.* There is no mention of Smith's illegal activities in the Harding Papers.

fied anti-administration crusade. Only the fact that Congress was not in session prevented these solons from filling the Capitol with emotional oratory. Instead, senators like Heflin and Caraway turned to a willing press to provide a temporary forum for their views, and they grandly predicted that the Veterans' Bureau investigation would be only "an opening round" in ferreting out gross malfeasance under Republican normalcy rule. Not to be outstripped by these Democratic prophecies, insurgent Republicans, especially LaFollette, told reporters that "anything might be expected" because of the control exerted over the Harding administration by "predatory interests."

In most respects, the Forbes investigation was a disappointment for these elements. Although the existence of corruption was proved beyond any doubt, no master plan for Forbes's chicanery was uncovered, nor did it seem that Forbes was a front man for anyone higher up in the administration. Apparently, his actions represented nothing but a patchwork of individual bribery and greed.[4]

Because the management and construction of all veterans' hospitals, as well as control over all medical supplies, were assigned to the Veterans' Bureau, Forbes certainly had ample opportunity to indulge in illegality. It all began in early 1922, when Forbes first met Elias H. Mortimer, an agent for the Thompson-Black Construction Company of St. Louis. Mortimer was extremely anxious to land hospital construction contracts for his firm, and during the winter of 1922 he often invited Forbes to visit him and his wife, Kathryn, in their Wardman Park Hotel apartment in Washington. In April, and again in June, the Mortimers accompanied Forbes on a hospital-site inspection tour of the West, during which Mortimer paid all the bills. While they were in St. Louis, Mortimer set up a meeting between Forbes and John W. Thompson, one of the firm's owners, at which time Forbes received a $5,000 "loan" in exchange for preferential treatment for the Thompson-Black company.

4. Basic information on Forbes and the Veterans' Bureau is in *Investigation of Veterans' Bureau,* Hearings before the Select Committee, U.S. Senate, 67th Congress, 4th Session (Washington, D.C., 1923).

Simultaneously, Forbes worked out an arrangement with the Hurley-Mason Construction Company of Tacoma (which was owned by a friend of Forbes) whereby the two firms would engage in a closed system of bidding so that all profits from the building of hospitals would be split three ways: one-third to Thompson-Black, one-third to Hurley-Mason, and one-third to Forbes. Concurrently, Forbes also speculated on land sites for the hospitals, authorizing the government to pay exorbitant prices for land that was worth only a fraction of the cost. The difference was divided between Forbes and the bureau's chief counsel, Cramer, who arranged the site deals.

In November 1922, Forbes initiated yet another scheme for defrauding the government. Stored in some fifty buildings at the medical-supply depot at Perryville, Maryland, were huge quantities of surplus materials—sheets, towels, drugs, gauze, pajamas, moleskin, liquor, and even hardware and a few trucks. Some of these items had been damaged during storage because of leaky roofs, and Forbes arranged for a Boston firm, Thompson and Kelley, to make a bid ostensibly on these damaged goods. Other items, however, were surreptitiously covered in the bid, since on November 15 Forbes signed a contract turning over to Thompson and Kelley undamaged supplies worth $3 million for only $600,000.

Although it was this deal that caused Forbes's confrontation with Harding in February 1923, it was Elias Mortimer who finally decided his fate. Forbes's attentions to Kathryn Mortimer in the spring and summer of 1922 had made Mortimer suspicious, and when his wife later left him, he blamed Forbes for her desertion. In seeking revenge, Mortimer was more than willing to talk to the Senate investigating committee.

Mortimer's disclosures of corruption in the Veterans' Bureau were contested by Forbes, who, in November 1923, returned from Europe and appeared before the committee in his own behalf. However, his testimony was totally unconvincing, and he and John W. Thompson were bound over for trial in Chicago in 1924 for conspiracy to defraud the government. Neither

Forbes nor Thompson took the stand in his own defense, and the jury required only a brief deliberation to find both defendants guilty. Receiving a two-year jail sentence and a $10,000 fine, Forbes began his term at Leavenworth on March 21, 1926. Thompson, because of a bad heart, never served his two-year sentence, and died in St. Louis on May 3, 1926.

The Veterans' Bureau scandal was hardly news when a more sensational plan to cheat the government made the headlines. Growing out of the activities of Albert Fall as secretary of the interior, this situation was complicated by honest differences between Fall and conservationists over a proper conservation policy. In most respects, Fall was an able cabinet officer. Hoover once characterized him as one of the best secretaries Interior ever had. But conservationists such as Gifford Pinchot, Commissioner of Forestry in Pennsylvania, and Henry A. Slattery, secretary of the National Conservation Association, believed Fall's anti-conservation attitudes more than offset his executive ability. These men constantly agitated for his removal.[5]

Their cries would have remained unheard were it not for a series of events that seemed to confirm their worst suspicions. In the spring of 1921, Fall convinced Secretary of the Navy Denby that the Interior Department could more suitably direct the long-range development of the naval oil reserves than the Navy Department. Upon the recommendation of Fall and with the written consent of Denby, President Harding in May 1921 transferred these reserves from the Navy Department to the Department of the Interior. Harding saw nothing insidious in this action, viewing it as merely an amicable adjustment between two cabinet officers over claims to a specific function. The order transferring the reserves was personally carried to the White House by Assistant Secretary of the Navy Theodore

5. For background on Fall and Teapot Dome, see Burl Noggle, "The Origins of the Teapot Dome Investigation," *MVHR*, XLIV, No. 2 (September 1957), 237–66; J. Leonard Bates, *The Origins of Teapot Dome: Progressives, Parties, and Petroleum, 1909–1921* (Urbana, Ill., 1963), especially 200–244.

Roosevelt, Jr., and had the tacit, if not enthusiastic, support of many naval officers.[6]

Conservationists saw the matter in a different light. Slattery immediately sought an audience with Assistant Secretary Roosevelt, who assured him that there was nothing to worry about. He then went to see Senator LaFollette and told him of his fear that Fall would give the oil reserves to private exploiters. Fall did indeed plan to develop the oil lands under the terms of the General Leasing Act of 1920, which permitted the private leasing of reserve land if it was thought to be in the national interest. In laying such plans, Fall was merely pursuing the course advocated earlier by Wilson's secretary of the interior, Franklin K. Lane, who strongly believed in the private development of government oil lands.

On July 12, 1921, the Interior Department granted a private lease in Naval Reserve No. 1, at Elk Hills, California, to the Edward L. Doheny oil interests. This award, duly reported in the press, resulted from open competitive bidding and elicited little comment. But during the next several months rumors circulated that other leases, secret and noncompetitive, were granted both in Elk Hills and in Naval Reserve No. 3, near Salt Creek, Wyoming, commonly called Teapot Dome. To quiet these rumors, Senator John B. Kendrick (Dem., Wyoming) asked the Interior Department for clarification, but received no answer. On April 15, 1922, therefore, he introduced a resolution in the Senate demanding an explanation.

At the time, Fall was on an inspection tour in the West, and the officer responsible for a reply was Acting Secretary Edward C. Finney. He admitted on April 18 that a lease to develop all of Teapot Dome had been granted to Harry F. Sinclair's Mammoth Oil Company, and that other leases in Elk Hills were pending for Doheny's Pan-American Petroleum and Transport Company. Three days later, Finney sent to the Senate a copy

6. A copy of the transfer order is in *Leases Upon Naval Oil Reserves,* Hearings before the Committee on Public Lands and Surveys, U.S. Senate, 68th Congress, 1st Session (Washington, D.C., 1924), I, 177–78.

of the Sinclair lease, along with an admission that there had been no competitive bidding because "national security and naval preparedness" were involved.

Conservationists such as Slattery and Pinchot immediately clamored for more information, but it was LaFollette who now assumed leadership of the conservation forces. LaFollette's interest was not so much in protecting the nation's oil reserves as in finding gaps in the administration's defenses and adding to its embarrassment. For LaFollette, attacking Fall was a means to an end, not an end in itself. Hence, on April 21 he introduced a new resolution, calling for additional clarification as to why no public announcement had been made and why a lease had been granted for all of Teapot Dome. A week later, sensing that the oil-lease question could be used not only as a powerful weapon against the administration but also as a way of enhancing his own budding presidential prospects, LaFollette modified his resolution to request an official inquiry by the Senate Committee on Public Lands and Surveys into *all* naval oil-reserve leases.[7]

After considerable persuasion by LaFollette, Democratic Senator Thomas J. Walsh of Montana agreed to assume responsibility for the investigation. A shrewd prosecutor, Walsh frankly did not think that LaFollette's crusade against Fall showed much promise. Besides, he was not sure of the purity of LaFollette's motives. Walsh noticed that most of the enthusiasm for the probe came from Republican insurgents on the Public Lands Committee—Ladd, Norbeck, and Norris—men who were constantly lambasting the executive and vying with the White House for control of their own party. Still, the investigation also afforded the Democrats a chance to harass the Republicans, and therefore Walsh accepted the job, primarily as a party duty.

Walsh at first found his task as unenlightening as he had expected, especially after Fall dumped a mass of material on him concerning the leases, including a letter from Harding dated

7. Unless otherwise noted, subsequent data concerning the Teapot Dome scandal are from *Leases Upon Naval Oil Reserves.*

June 7, 1922, which said that the Fall-Denby oil policy "was submitted to me prior to the adoption thereof, and the policy decided upon and the subsequent acts have at all times had my entire approval." But there were just enough events of a suspicious nature during the fall and winter of 1922–23 to keep Walsh at his task. Sometime after the LaFollette resolution was passed, the Wisconsin senator's office was ransacked and, later, Walsh's own past in Montana was secretly checked. Moreover, there were indications that his phones were being tapped and that his mail was being opened. Walsh also began to receive all sorts of information about illegal leasing negotiations and alleged "oil deals." [8]

Secretary Fall, meanwhile, resigned from the cabinet, claiming that he needed to devote more time to his private business affairs. It was known that Fall was unhappy over his declining influence with Harding, and his resignation on March 4, 1923, did not cause surprise or arouse suspicion. It was interesting, however, that immediately after his resignation he accepted employment with the Sinclair oil interests and accompanied Harry Sinclair to Russia to arrange for oil concessions there.

Harding gave no evidence during this period of suspecting Fall of illegal activities, and his letter to the Walsh committee in June 1922 was not an attempt to cover up skulduggery but the natural reaction of a president who wished to support a presumably faithful but beleaguered subordinate. Harding regarded the congressional attacks on Fall in 1922–23, especially by LaFollette, as being politically inspired, and believed that Fall, like Daugherty, was often falsely maligned and bore the brunt of much criticism that otherwise would have been directed at him. [9]

8. Walsh's papers clearly reveal his motives in handling the investigation and contain many letters urging him to take the job. His papers also contain many examples of the kind of rumors and information that came to him. Thomas J. Walsh Papers (LC), Boxes 208–14.

9. William Allen White claimed that Harding knew all about Fall, and created a highly fictionalized encounter between Harding and Mrs. Fall in Kansas City during Harding's western trip to prove it. Daugherty in *The Inside Story*, 202, unequivocally states that Harding did not know about Fall. All available evidence, including the Harding Papers, supports Daugherty.

Harding was dead, of course, when on October 24, 1923, just two days after the Veterans' Bureau investigation began, Fall appeared as a lead-off witness in the oil investigation. Walsh opened the hearings even though he did not yet have anything specific against Fall. As a result, the early sessions were mere fishing expeditions, with Walsh getting the worst of it. Fall seemed supremely confident, took full responsibility for his actions, claimed that naval security required discretion in publicizing the leases, asserted that before his resignation he had never been in either Sinclair's or Doheny's employ, and swore that he had never received any money from them while he was in government service. Although some subsequent witnesses, such as Secretary Denby, appeared less self-assured—and even scared—there were no contradictions in testimony. And when both Doheny and Sinclair, under oath, confirmed Fall's claims—namely, that he had not received any benefits, directly or indirectly, as a result of awarding the leases—most observers were convinced that the oil investigation had reached a dead end.

Then came a break. Through information received from New Mexico, it became known that Fall had recently spent more than $100,000 in improving his ranch there and in buying adjacent land. Moreover, it was discovered that during the period of the lease negotiations Sinclair had visited Fall's ranch and had sent him a few head of blooded Holstein cattle and two prize hogs. Fall, who at the time of these disclosures was at his New Mexico ranch, was ordered to reappear before the committee and explain these contacts with Sinclair and his sudden prosperity. Returning to Washington in late December 1923, Fall secluded himself in the Wardman Park Hotel, reiterated his innocence in a letter to the committee and claimed that his sudden affluence had come through a $100,000 loan from the newspaper millionaire Edward B. McLean, but pleaded that his "poor health" made it impossible for him to appear and answer questions under oath.

Walsh summarily ordered McLean to testify. But McLean was vacationing in Palm Beach, Florida, and sent word that his "bad sinuses" prevented him from coming to Washington and taking the stand. Walsh therefore went to Palm Beach and, as a subcommittee of one, queried the newspaper owner about the Fall loan. McLean finally denied making such a loan. Still in seclusion in the Wardman Park Hotel, Fall now admitted in a new letter to the committee that he had not received the money from McLean after all but from "other sources." He refused to divulge these sources but vehemently denied that the money had come from either Sinclair or Doheny.

Other disclosures now came thick and fast, but none was as sensational as the subsequent testimony of Edward Doheny. On January 24, 1924, this little sixty-seven-year-old oil millionaire and former prospector friend of Albert Fall stepped again before the committee and stated that it was he who had "loaned" the New Mexican the $100,000, not because of any interest in oil leases but because of their "old friendship." This sum, Doheny said, "was a bagatelle to me . . . no more than $25 or $50 perhaps to the ordinary individual." According to Doheny, the money had been delivered to Fall in November 1921 by his son, Edward, Jr., in a little black satchel. "It was my own money," he added, "and did not belong in whole or in part to any oil company with which I am connected." For that reason, Doheny said, what he had told the committee earlier was still true—that Fall had not profited in any way from the oil leases.

The committee, however, found this difficult to believe, especially since ensuing testimony from others revealed that Fall had also received an undetermined number of Liberty bonds from Sinclair. Angered by the committee's skepticism, Doheny once again returned to the stand, and this time bluntly stated that Fall was not the only government official with whom he had monetary dealings in his life. He reminded the committee that over the years he had contributed as heavily to the Democratic party as to the Republican party and stated that several former members of Wilson's cabinet—William G. McAdoo, Franklin K. Lane, Thomas W. Gregory, and A. Mitchell Palmer

—had been on his payroll at one time or another. "I paid them for their influence," snapped Doheny.

In view of these disclosures, it became absolutely imperative that Fall testify, and, despite his continued protests that he was too ill to take the stand, a subpoena was issued to force his presence. On February 2, Fall finally appeared in a jam-packed Senate caucus room—a trembling wreck, leaning on a cane, wearing a wrinkled and baggy suit, his shoulders sagging, his mouth drooping, and his gold-framed glasses hanging limply from his ears. Looking more worried than ill, and with eyes downcast, he read: "I decline . . . to answer any questions on the ground that it may tend to incrim:nate me." [10]

The immediate result of all this furor was a further polarization of American politics and a Roman holiday of press sensationalism. From the first intimation of sudden prosperity on Fall's New Mexico ranch, the press ran story after story on the Teapot Dome situation, evaluating, elucidating, analyzing, and exaggerating every rumor and every scrap of evidence. As a result, the average citizen came to believe that the entire government was riddled with the "oil scandals." While the smell of oil money hung in the air, journalistic sleuths trailed its odor in every direction. Where the smell did not exist, they often created it. Especially did the press revel in the political reputations tarnished by oil. The final Doheny disclosures gave rise to wild press speculation on the extent to which all public officials, Republicans and Democrats alike, were involved. Gross exaggerations about the "evil and insidious connections" between big business and government became commonplace. The liberal press in particular had a field day, decrying the "easy corruptibility" of conservatives such as Fall and using Teapot Dome as a morality lesson for all Americans.

If the press was agitated by the oil scandal, politicians were even more exercised. Politicians of all stripes seized upon the event for partisan purposes. At first, Republicans were on the

10. For the most dramatic description of this moment, see Sullivan, *Our Times,* VI, 329.

defensive, anxiously parrying Democratic thrusts and worrying about how deep the roots of the scandal lay. Democrats, of course, found Teapot Dome a much more effective weapon to use against their Republican adversaries than the Veterans' Bureau affair. With Congress again in session, these solons now enthusiastically appropriated Teapot Dome in their drive for party advantage and purposely magnified the scandal out of all proportion. Initially, the storm centered only on Secretary Fall. But as time went by, Fall became simply a stand-in for the executive branch of government as a whole. An amazing amount of the congressional vehemence directed at Fall was bipartisan in nature and obviously sprang from general congressional frustration with the two preceding presidents. Harding's growing independence and direct challenges to congressional authority were highly reminiscent of Wilson's activities and left many congressmen with a desire to strike back at the White House. Fall now presented them with that opportunity as well as the occasion to offer a stern warning to Harding's successor. Many congressmen had felt themselves put on trial by Harding's western speeches, and they had suffered badly under the lash of his effective moralizing about where the primary blame for the continuing executive-congressional tension lay. Therefore, Fall also became the instrument by which many of these congressmen, condemned first by Wilson and then by Harding for being selfish and blind to the national welfare, could refurbish their moral integrity.[11]

Under such circumstances, the House witnessed some interesting verbal gymnastics. But it was in the Senate that most of the action and the major confrontations occurred. There Democratic senators such as Caraway, Heflin, Harrison, and McKellar rattled the rafters with their denunciations and visited oratorical hellfire on their hapless pro-administration Republican colleagues. Republican insurgents like LaFollette and Norris

11. The various congressional comments on the oil scandal contained in *Congressional Record,* 68th Congress, 1st Session, are particularly revealing in their self-righteous tone and in their pointed attacks on "executive immorality and hypocrisy."

happily joined these Democrats in tirades of their own. Indeed, the oil scandal provided those in the progressive-oriented farm bloc with a triple opportunity. Not only could they denounce the executive branch and condemn what they believed to be anti-farm attitudes, but they could strike against big business at the same time. These men seized upon Fall's indiscretions as another example, like the Newberry case, of how business money was corrupting American politics. Furthermore, the oil scandal connected big business with one of the progressive movement's sacred tenets—conservation. This combination made old progressives like LaFollette tremble with excitement. Teapot Dome was a reconfirmation of all their earlier suspicions that big business was beyond redemption, and primed them for intensifying their crusade against the "vested interests." [12]

Doheny's testimony in late January slowed this drive somewhat by also casting doubt on the purity of some Democratic leaders and former progressives, especially McAdoo. Stung by these revelations, many Democrats, along with LaFollette and a few other insurgents, attempted to link other Republican cabinet members, and even Coolidge and Harding, with Fall's crimes. Some tried to connect Harding's "unexpected" nomination in 1920 with "oil deals" and Teapot Dome. When all these attempts failed, administration Republicans breathed a little easier and rebounded to strike back at their Democratic and insurgent tormentors both in and out of Congress. Since McAdoo was at the moment the leading Democratic contender for the 1924 nomination, and since Senator Walsh was one of his major supporters, the Republican counterassault centered on McAdoo's relationship with Doheny. In Congress, longtime McAdoo friends like Democratic Senator Carter Glass tried to defend him while Republican phrase-makers like Senator Moses claimed that McAdoo was just as "oily" as the rest.[13]

12. Again, the Senate debates in *Congressional Record,* 68th Congress, 1st Session, contain numerous examples of an anti-executive, anti-business, anti-administration bias.

13. Sample exchange over McAdoo in *Congressional Record,* 68th Congress, 1st Session, 2735–40.

While this intra- and inter-party sparring continued, a clamor arose from both Republicans and Democrats for President Coolidge to take decisive action to "clean up" the executive branch. Having already perceived that the Walsh investigation would provide no further embarrassing revelations concerning top Republican officials, Coolidge appointed in early February a special commission of two men—former Senator Atlee Pomerene (Dem., Ohio) and Owen J. Roberts, a lawyer from Philadelphia (Rep.)—to ascertain the full facts concerning Fall's "loans" and prepare the necessary prosecutions. Simultaneously, there were congressional demands that Secretary Denby resign, and shortly thereafter he volunteered his resignation, protesting his innocence but claiming that he would not tolerate prolonged congressional abuse.

The Roberts and Pomerene investigation ultimately revealed that Fall had received a total of about $400,000 from Sinclair and Doheny. Hence, in June 1924, Fall and Doheny were charged with conspiracy to defraud; Fall and Sinclair with conspiracy to defraud; and Fall and both Dohenys (father and son) with bribery. The resultant trials and legal maneuvering continued for almost six years. In the end, Sinclair served six months in jail for attempting to tamper with a jury, but was acquitted of all other charges. Doheny, too, was inexplicably acquitted of any wrongdoing. Only Fall suffered the consequences. Found guilty of accepting a bribe, he was sentenced to a year in jail and a $100,000 fine. He began serving his sentence in July 1931.

In late January 1924, Rollin Kirby, a cartoonist for the New York *World,* depicted a fat and sweaty GOP sitting in a chair and being forced to take a large dose of "Oil" from a huge spoon. The cartoon was captioned "Ugh!" and was an accurate description of the Republican party in the late winter and early spring of 1924.[14] However, distasteful as the oil issue proved to be, Teapot Dome served merely as the background for an even more determined attempt to uncover corruption in the govern-

14. New York *World,* January 30, 1924, cartoon.

ment and force a confrontation between Congress and the executive branch.

Not surprisingly, this one involved Harry Daugherty. Convinced that the Veterans' Bureau and Teapot Dome affairs were only the beginning of other sensational revelations, old Daugherty enemies slavered at the prospect of connecting the Attorney General with all this wrongdoing. But whatever Daugherty had to hide, it did not relate to Charles Forbes or Albert Fall. As we have seen, Daugherty did not like Forbes and helped expose him to Harding. Daugherty also disliked Fall, and the two men rarely conferred with one another. For example, Fall did not consult Daugherty on the legality of the oil leases or ask him about any leasing matter. Still, because all three men were friends of Harding, and because Daugherty was head of the Justice Department, which should have known about any irregularities, Daugherty was from the beginning inextricably linked with the others in the public, press, and congressional mind.

As could have been expected, no sooner had Secretary Denby resigned than voices were raised for Daugherty's removal. These demands reached a climax on February 19, 1924, when Senator Burton K. Wheeler (Dem., Montana) introduced a resolution calling for a thorough investigation of the Justice Department. The partisan intent behind this request was immediately betrayed by the unusual procedure of Wheeler's naming in his resolution himself and four others to serve on the investigating committee. Republican leaders were appalled by this turn of events. Having always regarded Daugherty as the administration's Achilles' heel anyway, they quailed at the thought of having to defend him. On February 20, a small group of them, including Lodge, called at the White House and begged Coolidge to force Daugherty's quick resignation. But Coolidge took no action and Daugherty hotly denied all charges.

Already infected by the intense emotionalism generated by the Veterans' Bureau and Teapot Dome affairs, the 68th Congress, which had convened in December 1923, now succumbed totally to investigation mania. Composed of members elected in the 1922 elections, this Congress contained elements that were bitterly hostile to the administration and especially to Daugherty, whose activities had provided one of the issues of the 1922 campaign. Labor representatives, in particular, lusted for Daugherty's blood, and even without the suspicion of scandal, the Attorney General would have received rough treatment from this Congress. As it was, anti-Daugherty plotters found their job easy, since they were now joined by other groups, mainly Democratic but including some Republicans, who relished the idea of not only "getting" Daugherty but undermining the entire "best minds" executive system.[15]

For over a week the proposed Wheeler resolution monopolized talk in congressional corridors and on the Senate floor as rumors, false statements, personal insults, and slander circulated, replacing reason and intelligent discussion. In this atmosphere, the Senate voted 66 to 1 on March 1 to adopt a revised resolution, which resembled Wheeler's except that it provided for the investigating committee to be elected from the floor. La-Follette immediately nominated Smith Brookhart (Rep., Iowa) as chairman; the other committee members nominated and elected were Wheeler (Dem., Montana), Jones (Rep., Washington), Moses (Rep., New Hampshire), and Henry F. Ashurst (Dem., Arizona). Brookhart's designation as chairman was especially significant. A rural demagogue, Brookhart was a product of the landslide in the West in 1922 and had made his debut in the Senate glorifying the farm and pillorying Wall Street. An ardent dry who drank only buttermilk, a strong supporter of the soldiers' bonus, and a vigorous opponent of ship subsidies, Brookhart had early called the Senate's attention to his middle name, which was Wildman. "It is my mother's name," he said, "but it is also notice to the standpatters that I am one Progressive who won't be tamed." [16]

15. The contemporary press from February 20 to March 2 was full of anti-Daugherty comments and assertions from congressmen, accompanied by sly innuendoes directed at the executive branch as a whole but especially at the White House and the cabinet.

16. Ray T. Tucker and Frederick R. Barkley, *Sons of the Wild Jackass* (Freeport, N.Y., 1969), 344.

During the process of selecting this committee, the Senate was exposed to the most outrageous vitriol and calumny. Charge after charge was fired off indiscriminately as Heflin, Caraway, Harrison, Wheeler, and others denounced administration leaders in general and Daugherty in particular. Daugherty, they asserted, was "capable of anything." It was common knowledge, they claimed, that he consorted with "crooks and gamblers," "low-life harpies," "profiteers," and "bribe-takers." In the upcoming investigation, roared Heflin, "the whole truth must be brought out." When Senator Simeon D. Fess of Ohio made a feeble attempt to neutralize these premature conclusions by defending Daugherty, the Bible-quoting Mississippian sneered, "By their fruits ye shall know them." [17] For men like Heflin, the investigation was already over.

Wheeler enthusiastically assumed the role of chief investigator for the committee and dominated the ensuing proceedings.[18] A freshman senator like Brookhart, Wheeler had been sworn in only four months before. Greedy for power and intensely ambitious politically, this forty-two-year-old newcomer saw a confrontation with Daugherty as his passport to fame. Having served once as a federal district attorney in Montana, Wheeler fancied himself a great prosecutor and relished the thought of bringing the Attorney General to his knees. Of liberal persuasion in the manner peculiar to the Northwest, Wheeler possessed an ill-disguised contempt for normalcy policies, considering them a sellout to eastern capitalists. Encouraged by the success of his fellow Montanan, Walsh, in the oil investigation, Wheeler hoped to duplicate his results in the case of the Justice Department.

But Wheeler was no Walsh. He acted first and thought afterward. He did not have Walsh's patience for detail or his sense of balance. Instead, sensationalism was Wheeler's watchword.

---

17. For typical comments, see *Congressional Record,* 68th Congress, 1st Session, 3301–11, 3317–26, 3398–3401, 3408–12.

18. For Wheeler's own account, which must be taken with a large grain of salt, see Burton K. Wheeler, *Yankee from the West* (New York, 1962).

When public hearings began on March 12, 1924, Wheeler called as his first witness Roxy Stinson, divorced wife of Jess Smith.[19] Wearing rimless glasses and looking like a schoolmarm —a contrived effect that enhanced the credibility of her testimony—Roxy told an amazing story. With the press hanging on every word, she recounted her relationship with the dead Smith, chronicled his fears the last time she saw him before his death, and alluded to "big deals" engineered by an "Ohio gang" at a "little green house on K Street." She claimed that Harry Daugherty knew all about this gang's activities and was in on the division of the spoils.

A parade of witnesses then followed, each telling of gross corruption and always linking Jess Smith with the action—and, through him, Harry Daugherty. Wheeler made the most of these disclosures, and whenever the connection between Smith and Daugherty was only implicit, he sought to make it explicit. Besides Roxy, Wheeler's other star witness was Gaston B. Means. Means connected Daugherty with the K Street operation and portrayed Smith as Daugherty's henchman. Means explained in detail the Ohio gang's procedures, the manner in which it secured clients, and how it arranged for payoffs. All in all, his testimony revealed a Justice Department riddled with corruption and an administration burdened with guilty knowledge of its activities.

From such testimony Wheeler extracted much sensationalism, but it remains questionable how much truth he gleaned. The fatal flaw in his investigation was the nature of his two important witnesses—Roxy Stinson, a divorcee of dubious motives, and Gaston Means, a known liar. Means was a confessed swindler and bootlegger who had once been indicted for murder.[20] Contrary to his testimony, he had not come into personal con-

19. Unless otherwise noted, the information on the Daugherty investigation is from *Investigation of the Honorable Harry M. Daugherty,* U.S. Senate Select Committee, 68th Congress, 1st Session (Washington, D.C., 1924).

20. A recent biography of Means that strives to separate truth from fiction is Edwin P. Hoyt, *Spectacular Rogue: Gaston B. Means* (Indianapolis, 1963).

tact with Harry Daugherty until March 1922, when rumors came to Daugherty that Means, having through fraud gained a position as an FBI agent, was involved in bribe-taking and liquor violations. Daugherty immediately suspended him from his job, eventually discharged him, and in 1923 secured indictments against him for conspiracy and bootlegging. These indictments were pending when Means gave his anti-Daugherty "testimony" before the Wheeler committee. As for Roxy, she was by her own admission a "disappointed woman" because Jess Smith, who left his estate to a number of persons, including Daugherty, had not made her sole legatee under his will. She was currently engaged in litigation to acquire all of Smith's assets and was being blocked by Daugherty.

Still, there was enough truth beneath the lies to justify some suspicion. In the end, it was the reaction of the Justice Department and of Daugherty himself to the investigation, rather than the disclosures, that proved really damaging. Throughout the inquiry, Wheeler was subjected by Justice Department agents to harassment, threats, espionage, and vilification. During the investigation, the rooms of committee witnesses were rifled, their papers were stolen, and pressure was put upon them not to testify. In early April, a trumped-up charge of bribery, initiated by the Justice Department, was even brought against Wheeler in an attempt to scare him off. This charge was so patently fraudulent that it was later laughed out of court.

Throughout this shabby affair, congressional voices demanding Daugherty's resignation became increasingly strident, and finally, on March 27, when Daugherty flatly refused to give the Wheeler committee access to Justice Department files, C. Bascom Slemp, Coolidge's private secretary, told Daugherty that the President expected his resignation. Daugherty reluctantly complied but pointedly reminded Coolidge: "I have not as yet had an opportunity to place upon the witness stand before the Senate Committee a single witness in my defense or in explanation or rebuttal of the whispered and gossipy charges against me." [21]

21. New York *Times,* March 29, 1924, p. 1, quoting Daugherty.

Once Daugherty's resignation was secured, there were second thoughts on the matter. Although virtually all journals agreed that Daugherty was "a misfit every day of the three years" he was in office, many deplored the fact that he had not been given an opportunity to defend himself. But apart from the question of individual justice, there was the matter of executive prerogatives. Even though Coolidge had not appointed Daugherty, the Attorney General was still a representative of the President, not of Congress. In Daugherty's case, Congress, specifically the Senate, was seeking to impose its will on the White House. Again, as in its assault on Fall and, to a lesser extent, on Denby, Congress's concern over corruption was matched by its desire to improve its position in relation to the presidency and to effect a loss in White House prestige. Coolidge, in turn, finally chose to capitulate to Congress on the Daugherty issue, partly because he had little love for Daugherty anyway but also because he was afraid not to. Courage was not a visible White House trait in the spring of 1924.

Congress, of course, rejoiced at Daugherty's dismissal. Democrats, maverick Republicans, and even many administration supporters expressed satisfaction at Coolidge's action. However, Daugherty's removal did not immediately restore congressional tranquillity or appease Congress's desire to flex its muscles. Instead, it served as the incentive for more wild charges and preposterous proposals. Senator McKellar promptly called for an investigation of Mellon, and hinted that after Mellon, Wallace and Hoover would be next. Cantankerous millionaire James ("Big Jim") Couzens of Michigan, who was currently fighting with the Treasury Department over his income taxes, enthusiastically assumed leadership of a drive to "get Mellon." Caraway was especially eager for Wallace's scalp, while Reed of Missouri itched to get "that internationalist," Herbert Hoover.[22]

Much of this sentiment flowed naturally from partisan po-

22. "Mr. Coolidge Dismisses Mr. Daugherty," *Nation*, CXVIII (April 9, 1924), 386; "Why Daugherty Is Out," *Literary Digest*, LXXX, No. 2 (April 12, 1924), 5–8.

litical animus. But again, some of it emanated from a deep-seated congressional urge to hobble the executive. That urge had been present in varying degrees in all congresses since 1918 and had shifted back and forth among Republicans and Democrats with considerable bipartisan impartiality. Neither party had a monopoly on it. The "irreconcilables" had displayed it in Wilson's day in their hatred of the White House and their absolute intransigency in foreign affairs. The farm bloc had shown such anti-executive bias in its various attitudes and actions in the Harding years, especially in its naked attempt in the Federal Reserve Board case to limit the presidential power of appointment. The Democrats revealed it most directly in the emotional and exaggerated nature of their assaults on Denby, Daugherty, and Fall. Now, with some insurgent Republican help, they sought to rid the government not only of the worst elements in the Harding executive legacy but also some of the very best. Indeed, if some of these congressmen had had their way in 1923–24, they would have used the scandals as the means of reducing the executive branch to the level of impotence of the Johnson administration in the post–Civil War era.

Fortunately, cooler heads prevailed and investigation hysteria finally passed without further damage to the executive branch or the nation. Democrats and insurgent Republicans were not able to muster allies enough to expand their anti-executive crusade, and, indeed, a backlash ultimately set in against them. As for the Justice Department investigation itself, the legal aftermath was inconclusive. Wheeler's slipshod methods and the questionable nature of the testimony resulted in only one successful prosecution. During the investigation, it was learned that Jess Smith had arranged through Colonel Thomas W. Miller, alien-property custodian, for the illegal transfer of an American subsidiary of a German-owned company to an American syndicate, which paid over $441,000 for this service. Subsequently, $50,000 of this amount found its way into the hands of Miller and $224,000 into the pocket of Jess Smith. Smith allegedly deposited $50,000 of his sum in a Washington Court House, Ohio, bank in an account called "Jess

Smith Extra No. 3," which was a political account used jointly by Smith and Harry Daugherty.

It was assumed that Daugherty was implicated in this payoff through "Jess Smith Extra No. 3," and therefore the Wheeler committee recommended that he, along with Miller, be indicted on charges of defrauding the government. Daugherty, however, continued to deny any wrongdoing and consistently claimed that Means and the other witnesses had lied, that he had never been in the "little green house on K Street," that he knew nothing about the activities of the "Ohio gang," and that Jess Smith's own corrupt behavior had not been known to him until just before Smith's death.

In his trial, held in September 1926, the crucial issue was Daugherty's exact connection with the "Jess Smith Extra No. 3" account. But when given the chance to take the stand and clear himself under oath, Daugherty instead wrote out and presented the following statement:

> Having been personal secretary for [Warren Harding and Mrs. Harding],
>
> And having been Attorney General of the United States during the time that President Harding served as President,
>
> And also for a time after President Harding's death under President Coolidge,
>
> And with all of those named as attorney, personal friend and Attorney General, my relations were of the most confidential character as well as professional,
>
> I refuse to testify and answer questions put to me. . . .[23]

As a result, the question of Daugherty's guilt had to be surrendered into the hands of the jury with the critical issue of "Jess Smith Extra No. 3" still unresolved. When the jury deadlocked, a retrial was ordered. At the second trial, held in 1927, the jury finally refused to convict Daugherty but found Miller guilty as charged. Miller ultimately served thirteen months in jail. All indictments against Daugherty were subsequently dropped.

Speculation over Daugherty's unwillingness to testify dom-

---

23. For the complete statement, see Sullivan, *Our Times,* VI, 354.

inated many a conversation in 1926–27. Certainly no other action Daugherty might have taken could have encouraged more rumors or been more damaging to his own and, in the long run, to Harding's personal reputation. Daugherty's most rabid Senate opponents, such as Heflin, darkly suggested that his refusal hid unspeakable crimes, and that Jess Smith had been murdered to conceal what he knew. Mark Sullivan, the newspaperman, did not believe that Daugherty's refusal related to corruption at all but to the protection of Harding's reputation, perhaps concerning some kind of "woman trouble." Daugherty's own lawyer, Max D. Steuer, hinted as much when, after the first trial, he told the press that nothing connected with the bribery case had impelled Daugherty to refuse to testify, and that if the jury knew the real reason "they would commend rather than condemn him." [24] As for Daugherty himself, he continued to insist that he had "done nothing that prevents my looking the whole world in the face." "If anybody does not like my position," he wrote a friend, "you can tell them to go to hell." [25]

Of course, Daugherty's unwillingness to testify at his trial raised again the whole question of the depth and extent of the various scandals and whether other individuals, including Harding himself, might not have been involved. But on the basis of all available evidence, this much seems clear. While Harding unquestionably had "woman trouble" and must bear the onus for that, he was not connected in any way with the political corruption that fouled his administration. Nor did he condone it. He certainly erred in appointing Charles Forbes to the Veterans' Bureau, and then compounded his mistake by allowing him to escape the country rather than face a congressional

24. *Ibid.*, 355. The "woman trouble" theory gained credence in 1927 with the publication of Nan Britton's famous book, *The President's Daughter,* in which she claimed to have had an illegitimate child by Harding at Asbury Park, New Jersey, in 1919. Harding's "woman trouble" represents a fascinating, yet sordid, story. For an analysis, see Murray, *The Harding Era,* 485–97, 528–33.

25. HMD to N. H. Fairbanks, April 3, 1924, Newton H. Fairbanks Papers (OHSL).

showdown. When Harding became suspicious of Smith's activities, he moved to break all contact with him and effect his banishment from Washington. But again, he was not able to take the kind of drastic action that the situation obviously called for. Harding did not suspect Albert Fall, nor did he ever express any doubts about Daugherty. Because of the partisan congressional attacks made on these two men, he regarded them both as martyrs to normalcy policies rather than evil influences infecting his regime. As for Daugherty, he was not involved in Smith's corrupt activities in any direct way, and throughout 1926–27 was sincerely striving to protect the dead president's personal reputation as much as his own.

Nor was Harding's cabinet culpable with regard to the scandals. The question of the oil leases was never brought before the cabinet for discussion. The activities of Albert Fall remained hidden from other cabinet members, and they were as surprised as the rest of the country when Fall's various "loans" were uncovered. Secretary Hughes frankly asserted that he was unaware of any corruption; so did other cabinet officers. Even Hoover, who knew more about the internal workings of the Harding government than anyone else, said that he never suspected any wrongdoing. This was probably correct. As we have seen, each Harding cabinet officer conducted the business of his department without interference from the others, and each reported to the cabinet as a whole only in a general way. This procedure not only allowed corruption to go undetected but may even have encouraged it. Certainly a member who was morally weak could easily take advantage of the situation, as Secretary Fall obviously did.

With respect to the scandals themselves, corruption was definitely not inherent in the philosophy of normalcy or an inevitable outgrowth of it. Teapot Dome, for example, was not the broadly conceived, sinister plot to bargain away the nation's resources that some congressmen and later writers, such as William Allen White, contended. Instead, it was a relatively unsophisticated operation engineered by one man whose greed caused him to do business for the government as he might have done it for a private corporation—negotiate with companies he believed best qualified to do the job, arrange a suitable bargain with them, and collect a fat fee on the side for his trouble.

As for the mysterious "Ohio gang," it, too, was not part of a grand, integrated scheme to plunder the government, as Bruce Bliven, a liberal journalist who popularized the theory, persistently claimed. Nor was Harry Daughtery, despite the implication of "Jess Smith Extra No. 3," its mastermind and leader. The gang was simply a loose grouping of petty grafters around the vain and deluded Smith. Composed of Smith; Howard Mannington, an Urbana, Ohio, newspaper editor; Fred A. Caskey, a minor politician from Marietta, Ohio; and M. P. Kraffmiller, a friend of Caskey's from Illinois, the gang ran the "little green house on K Street" as a kind of racket headquarters. Contrary to later exaggerations, affairs there were not rowdy but commercial, and aroused no suspicion from the neighbors. Mannington and Caskey handled most of the action, but Jess Smith came around to grab his share of the profits and arrange for any "big stuff," such as immunity from prosecution or deals requiring access to Justice Department stationery or files. Through his association with Daugherty, Smith had the run of the Justice Department and turned this privilege to the gang's advantage.

Peddling influence, selling liquor permits, and arranging for the illegal sale of government property, this group did a brisk business. Yet it was a haphazard operation requiring no cohesion and based on no plan. The various members of the gang hung together only as a matter of expediency, and each was extremely jealous and distrustful of the other. They sought the quick deal, not sustained graft. Division of the profits occurred on an unscheduled and unregulated basis. In brief, compared with the great bosses and professional grafters in American history, the men in the Ohio gang were amateurs and their take was small.

The rhetoric of any event is usually a distortion of reality. This was certainly true of the rhetoric of corruption in the early 1920s. In place of the unadorned and comparatively unsensational truth, rumor fed rumor concerning the nature of the various Harding scandals, and constant exaggeration bred misinterpretations that, in turn, were breathlessly and universally repeated. Anti-administration elements within the Republican party invited the use of such misinterpretations against the leadership in their own party and actively aided the manufacture of exaggerations in their struggle with the executive over priorities and program development. The Democrats added their voices to the cacophony, hoping that the din and confusion would drown their own intense partisan desire to undermine their Republican opponents as they strove to regain national power. Congressmen in general, smarting from the various ignominies of the Wilson period as well as from the battles of the Harding years, embroidered skillfully on the worst exaggerations about the activities of the executive branch, openly enjoying its dismay and discomfort. In such manner, myths concerning the early years of normalcy were not only created but encouraged to grow. And as journalists and contemporary writers—the most articulate being pro-Wilson and partial to the Progressive Era—wrote down their "impressionistic" views of the 1920s, these myths finally acquired through repetition an aura of veracity. Visibly affected by the yellow journalism of the day, these observers found it particularly difficult to eschew the spectacular and the dramatic in their reporting. Just as they groped for colorful epithets to describe a golfer like Bobby Jones or a baseball player like Babe Ruth, so they sought similarly to characterize a politician such as Harding. To them, Jones was the Galileo of the Links, Ruth the Sultan of Swat, and Harding the King of Scandals.

Such rhetoric, unfortunately, prompted later and more seasoned commentators on the American scene also to indulge in glittering generalities and led them to faulty conclusions concerning the nature of the early 1920s and the beginning of normalcy. At their hands, normalcy and scandal became virtually synonymous. They persistently condemned the one by means of the other. It was clearly a case of guilt by association. No serious attempt was made to examine the period impartially, to diagnose contemporary antagonisms, to analyze motivations, to evaluate political results, or, most important, to withhold moral judgment. Consequently, millions of history students as well as their teachers came to accept and transmit wholly exaggerated and erroneous ideas about the era. Some corruption existed, to be sure, but it was not the most significant aspect of this period of American history. The story of Babylon was not, as William Allen White later piously asserted, a Sunday-school story compared with the early normalcy years.[26]

Yet, the historical record notwithstanding, for most Americans the scandals remained, and still remain, the most memorable facet of that era. The rhetoric of corruption continues to do its work.

26. Walter Johnson, ed., *Selected Letters of William Allen White, 1899–1943* (New York, 1947), 260.

6

The Legacy

WHEN President Calvin Coolidge issued his first official proc-
lamation on August 4, 1923, formally announcing Harding's
death, the nation did not know what to expect from this new
leader. Coolidge had not been visible during the Harding years.
Except for presiding over the Senate, he had not participated in
policy-making nor had he been close to any cabinet officer.
Harding had not relied on him at all and thought of him simply
as "that little fellow from Massachusetts." Indeed, as early as
1922, party leaders were speculating that Harding might dump
Coolidge for another running mate in 1924. Certainly there was
no expectation that he would succeed to the presidency.[1]

Coolidge's sudden succession, therefore, drastically altered
the political situation and sent both politicians and the nation's news media scurrying to find new touchstones. The press,
which had previously ignored the vice-president, underwent
an amazing metamorphosis. Newspaperman Clinton Gilbert
later recalled: "In a week the only thing there was in common
between Mr. Coolidge, the Vice-President, and Mr. Coolidge,
the President, was his name." According to Thomas L. Stokes,
another newspaperman: "It was one of the greatest feats of
newspaper propaganda that the modern world has seen. It was
really a miracle. He said nothing. Newspapers must have copy.

---

1. Coolidge's various biographers have created a myth concerning
his usefulness to the Harding administration. Claude M. Fuess, for example, in his *Calvin Coolidge: The Man from Vermont* (Boston, 1940)
claims that Harding thought highly of Coolidge and consulted with him
frequently. Fuess was wrong on both counts.

So we grasped little incidents to build up human interest stories and we created a character." [2]

Certain aspects of the Coolidge personality fitted neatly into the desired image. After the onset of the scandals, the presidential office badly needed bolstering, and Coolidge's idiosyncrasies, ridiculed at an earlier time, now became virtues. Being less gregarious and affable than Harding, Coolidge immediately tempered the open atmosphere surrounding the White House, and this "change" was heralded by the press as a conscious effort to eliminate the "carousing" that had occurred during the Harding years. Given the personal interests of the new president, this shift would have happened anyway. In any case, Coolidge wisely and quietly accepted the accolades for his "good judgment" and proceeded to attach to the presidential office his kind of puritanism, which quickly restored national respect but was hardly exciting.

Most observers failed to perceive, or chose to ignore, the fact that this Coolidge "change" extended only to superficialities and not to personnel or to programs. For the moment, the "best minds" cabinet was kept intact, and when change did occur (the resignations of Denby and Daugherty), it was forced by congressional and public opinion, not by Coolidge. Coolidge retained all Harding appointees on regulatory boards and commissions, and even reappointed Dr. Sawyer as White House physician. The only major voluntary resignation following Harding's death was that of George Christian as the President's private secretary. He left to handle Mrs. Harding's personal affairs.

As for policies, Coolidge's position was crystal clear. At his first cabinet meeting on August 14, 1923, he stated that *all* the Harding policies, not just some of them, would be continued. Two weeks later, at a press conference, he reiterated this position, and in his first message to Congress, in December 1923, he repeated it again. In short, Coolidge early staked his political future on the normalcy program. Among the policies he

2. Clinton W. Gilbert, *You Takes Your Choice* (New York, 1924), 27; Thomas L. Stokes, *Chip Off My Shoulder* (Princeton, 1940), 139.

reendorsed were the collection of all war debts, further restriction of immigration, maintenance of protection for American industry, additional credit legislation for the farmer, the continuation of economy in government, opposition to the soldiers' bonus, and the return of shipping to private ownership. He even announced his support for membership in the World Court. Not one step did Coolidge stray from the Harding path. But because of the scandals, the press totally ignored this fact and talked instead of Coolidge's "constructive policy," his "sound program," and his "emergent wise leadership."

For the remainder of Harding's unexpired term, Coolidge's performance was as good as his promise. He formally repeated Harding's request to the Senate to accept membership on the World Court. He encouraged the negotiation of more World War I debt-funding agreements. He urged Secretary of Labor Davis to overhaul the immigration system, and he endorsed the 1924 Johnson immigration bill. He upheld Mellon in his continuing efforts to reduce the national debt. He strongly supported the Budget Bureau. And on the bonus question he was even more obdurate than Harding. Coolidge would not countenance a bonus with or without proper funding, and in mid-May 1924, when the 68th Congress passed a renewed bonus law, he immediately vetoed it.

Throughout this period, Coolidge, like his predecessor, continued to experience extreme difficulty with Congress as that body's anti-executive attitudes reached full flower. LaFollette, whose presidential aspirations were quickening, spurred Republican mavericks into persistent confrontation with the new president. Since this group usually held the balance of power, it successfully blocked most administration action by means of a coalition with Democrats. In the first four months after Coolidge's December 1923 message, the 68th Congress did not act favorably on a single executive proposal, spending its time engaging in name-calling and in investigation hysteria instead. When it did act, it clearly showed its disdain for the White House. It peremptorily passed the soldiers' bonus over Coolidge's veto. It drastically altered a new Mellon tax plan. And, in order to reassert congressional prerogatives, it argued, often ridiculously, about the qualifications of the President's nominations for replacements for Denby and Daugherty (Curtis D. Wilbur and Harlan F. Stone, respectively, were finally endorsed). By early summer, most political observers felt sorry for Coolidge, and there was general relief when the first session of the 68th Congress adjourned in June to make way for the nominating conventions and the 1924 presidential campaign.

Of course, Coolidge's relationship with Congress was additionally complicated by the scandals. Coolidge had to satisfy congressional moralists by appearing pure himself while at the same time heading a party that was obviously tainted by corruption. Fortunately, with regard to the scandals, there was ultimately a limit to public, and even congressional, credulity. As we have already seen, throughout the winter months of 1924 the entire nation wallowed in the muck churned up by the various investigations. But by late March the public had gradually ceased to be preoccupied by the scandals, and even became wearied by them. By late April, as Wheeler failed to deliver on his numerous promises of new revelations of an "almost unbelievable nature" in the Justice Department investigation, public interest not only lapsed but turned against him. Both Wheeler and Walsh began to receive complaints about their "grandstanding." By May 8, not a single spectator attended the dying Teapot Dome hearings. In June, when the final Walsh report implicated only Fall, Sinclair, and Doheny in the oil affair, it was greeted in many quarters with derision. One editor remarked that after all the thunder and earthquake the report was like a "still small voice." Another concluded: "The single, solemn truth is that the Walsh report is a flat fizzle." [3]

Coolidge, by doing nothing more during this period than appointing a two-man council and placing Daugherty's head on a congressional platter, emerged virtually unscathed. What he

3. *Literary Digest,* LXXXI (June 21, 1924), 14–15; *American Federationist,* XXXI (July 1924), 577–78. The Walsh report is *Leases Upon Naval Oil Reserves,* 68th Congress, 1st Session, Senate Report No. 794 (Washington, D.C., 1924).

may have lost temporarily in presidential authority by giving in to Congress on the Daugherty issue he more than recouped by allowing Congress to continue to make a fool of itself unaided. By remaining quiet and unobtrusive, whether by calculation or mere inclination, Coolidge let the fires of public discontent, without which no congressional attack on the executive could be successful, burn out of their own accord. There were a number of factors aiding him. Already predisposed to view Congress suspiciously because of the squabbles during the Harding years, the public saw in the actions of some congressional leaders (especially Wheeler and LaFollette) the telltale signs of self-serving activity. Too, the public's sense of morality had been blunted by the war, and a little cheating by government officials seemed tame when compared with earlier wartime profiteering. Besides, it was difficult to sustain public interest in a few examples of government graft when the nation was currently caught up in more sensational events, such as the Leopold and Loeb murder of Bobby Franks, which the insatiable press blew up into earth-shaking proportions.

But of all the factors causing a decline in public interest, none was so important as the return of business prosperity. By the spring of 1924, solid evidence of spiraling profits and increased sales was competing with the scandal disclosures for the front pages of the newspapers. Such proof of an expanding economy not only helped mute anti-administration sentiment in Congress but encouraged further defections in the nation's middle and upper-middle classes from the reform tenets of progressivism—a process that World War I, the effects of Wilsonism, and the postwar depression had already begun. Many such defectors now rapidly embraced normalcy policies, and especially the new philosophy of welfare capitalism that sprang from them. Paradoxically, therefore, if Harding left to his successor the awesome liability of the scandals, he also gave him an overriding asset in the emerging success of the normalcy program as reflected in a rising economy.

The importance of this legacy was nowhere more apparent than in the presidential election of 1924. Actually, the 1924

campaign began in 1922, while Harding was still alive. The results of the fall congressional elections of that year caused
Democrats and anti-administration elements to assume falsely
that the normalcy program was unacceptable to the voting public. As a result, within the Democratic party there was a sudden
stirring among such potential presidential contenders as Mc-
Adoo, Underwood, and Al Smith. LaFollette, meanwhile, confident that his own hazy rural progressivism could be substituted
for normalcy, moved inexorably toward throwing his hat in the
ring. Throughout 1923 and 1924, labor men, old Populists,
single-taxers, Bull Moosers, intellectuals, and some Socialists
fed the Wisconsin senator's presidential ambitions by urging him
to run on either a third-party or an independent ticket. The real
base of LaFollette's support, however, remained with the insurgent "aggies," who by mid-1924 had effected a complete break
with the White House. Such agrarian insurgency did not have a
broad national appeal, and most of the insurgents, instead of
possessing a truly enlightened political philosophy, embraced
a hodgepodge of unsophisticated and outmoded beliefs based
on farm slogans and rural idioms of the late nineteenth century.

Using the scandals and the probable unavailability of Mc-
Adoo, because of the Doheny disclosures, as an excuse, La-
Follette "allowed" himself to be nominated by a convention of
the so-called Progressive Party in Cleveland in July 1924.[4] As
his running mate, he hand-picked Senator Wheeler, who by mid-
1924 found the Democratic party no longer big enough to contain his ambitions. The LaFollette-Wheeler platform, written
personally by LaFollette and read to the convention by his son,
condemned Mellon and his tax philosophy, denounced protective tariffs, favored the soldiers' bonus, called for the abolition
of the injunction in labor disputes, and rejected the current
"mercenary trends" in American foreign policy. In brief, La-
Follette's position represented a frontal challenge to normalcy
policies and an indictment of the conservative attitudes upon

---

4. The Robert M. LaFollette Papers (LC) for the years 1923–24
reveal the desire of LaFollette to gain the presidency, although that desire is submerged in a considerable amount of self-righteous rhetoric.

which they rested. In the eyes of LaFollette, Harding was still running in 1924, not Coolidge. Coolidge was merely the custodian of the normalcy program.[5]

Coolidge was not ashamed to run on that program. And from the beginning, he contrived it so that no one else should have the chance. To discourage other Republican hopefuls, such as Hiram Johnson, from making the race, Coolidge formally announced his candidacy as early as December 8, 1923. Thereafter, Republican leaders and top government officials one by one offered him their support. By mid-April, he held firm pledges from enough delegates to capture the nomination. Under these circumstances, the Republican convention, held in mid-June 1924, was anticlimactic. Skillfully organized by Coolidge's manager, William M. Butler, the gathering quickly nominated him and reaffirmed the normalcy platform of 1920. For a running mate, the convention significantly settled on Charles Dawes, a man whom Harding had once mentioned as his own successor and who even at the height of the scandals had refused to turn his back on the dead president.

As a candidate, Coolidge possessed certain obvious advantages, which have been the subject of much discussion by historians—his integrity, his taciturnity, his sense of timing. But of paramount significance was Coolidge's decision, despite the scandals, to stand on the normalcy program. Coolidge counted on the fact that the elections of 1922 had not indicated a trend against normalcy but, as Harding had said, represented merely a general dissatisfaction because prosperity had not yet returned. With prosperity now returning, normalcy seemed to offer the winning combination. Besides, by sticking with the normalcy program, Coolidge automatically secured the support of all former pro-Harding men and kept the Republican party intact except for the loss of a few die-hard insurgents who were badly disaffected anyway. More important, the same general

5. Kenneth C. MacKay's *The Progressive Movement of 1924* (New York, 1947) is still the best book on the 1924 campaign. Despite the efforts of Fola and Belle C. LaFollette in their *Robert M. LaFollette* (2 vols., New York, 1953), a first-rate biography of the Wisconsin senator remains to be written.

party organization that had swept Harding to an overwhelming victory in 1920 now became a factor in keeping Coolidge in the White House.

The Democrats were hopelessly divided in 1924. Besides possessing too many "favorite sons" who hoped to ride into the White House on a wave of public indignation against the scandals, the party by 1924 was badly split between its northern urban wing and its conservative southern and southwestern element. It is significant that Democratic opposition to normalcy policies during the years 1921–24 had not provided the party with a sufficiently strong bond to hold its ranks together. The Democrats, of course, were afflicted by the same kind of occupational and regional economic pressures that divided the Republicans. But unlike the Republicans, whose split was almost exclusively an east-west division and centered on economic issues, the Democrats also suffered from emerging cultural and ideological differences symbolized by its northern urban element. The Democratic party by 1923–24 was beginning to argue openly about such non-economic and "non-political" matters as prohibition, religious qualifications for office, and the Ku Klux Klan. Hoping to paper over this chaotic disunity, the Democratic convention selected Senator Walsh as permanent chairman and filled Madison Square Garden with howls of delight as Senator "Pat" Harrison in his keynote address concentrated on the saturnalia of Republican corruption in Washington. But Republican corruption was about the only issue around which all Democrats could rally. The chastening experience of 103 ballots to nominate John W. Davis, a conservative lawyer and former ambassador to Great Britain, as their presidential candidate was followed by ideological trauma as Charles W. Bryan, a western radical and brother of William Jennings Bryan, was selected as Davis's running mate. As one wag said, by this action the Democrats succeeded in "snatching defeat from the jaws of victory." [6]

6. The antics of this convention are fully contained in *Official Report of the Proceedings of the Democratic National Convention . . . 1924* (Indianapolis, 1924).

Actually, victory was never in sight for anyone other than Coolidge. The LaFollette alternative proved unacceptable to the public, while the Democrats failed to offer any alternative at all. Davis conducted a lackluster campaign, displaying no ingenuity or drive. Hampered by poor organization and by internal party strife, the Democrats foundered early in the campaign and never recovered.[7] LaFollette, meanwhile, flailed wildly about, mouthed old Populist shibboleths, experienced trouble in keeping even his farm support in line, and finally succumbed to the same regional and class parochialism that had defeated other third-party movements.[8]

Surprisingly, in the one area where the Republicans were the most vulnerable—the scandals—neither the Progressives nor the Democrats mounted a sustained attack. The Democrats were increasingly embarrassed by their own indirect involvement through Lane, McAdoo, and others, and they generally skirted the subject. The Progressives were more aggressive, especially Wheeler, who rarely missed an opportunity to tell audiences of his "intimate knowledge" of Republican corruption. LaFollette, however, was usually too busy condemning Wall Street for its "gigantic robberies" to be bothered with such peripheral thievery as that committed by Miller and Fall. The Republicans, meanwhile, met the scandal issue with silence. Coolidge believed that no candidate was ever injured by talking too little; hence, he made only a few set speeches and spent the remainder of the time quietly working at his desk in Washington.[9]

Long before the voters went to the polls, it was clear that

7. The John W. Davis Papers in the Sterling Memorial Library of Yale University clearly show the futility and disorganization of the Democratic campaign.

8. Again, the LaFollette Papers (LC), especially Series B, containers 98–102 and 119, are most revealing concerning LaFollette's philosophy, campaign tactics, and White House aspirations.

9. Burl Noggle, in his *Teapot Dome: Oil and Politics in the 1920's* (Baton Rouge, 1962), viii, claims that Teapot Dome was actually more of a liability for the Democrats than for the Republicans. See also J. Leonard Bates, "The Teapot Dome Scandal and the Election of 1924," *AHR*, LX, No. 2 (January 1955), 303–22.

Coolidge would win. By late October, the *Literary Digest* claimed that Coolidge would outstrip his nearest rival by more than two to one. The prediction was not far wrong. Of the 28,647,000 votes cast on election day, Coolidge received 15,-275,000; Davis 8,385,000; and LaFollette 4,826,000. Thus, in a three-way race, Coolidge collected 54 percent, a spectacular showing. Thirty-five states gave him 382 electoral votes, while Davis gathered 136 and LaFollette only 13 (Wisconsin). Despite later attempts to play up LaFollette's vote, his showing was poor. Of his total vote, approximately 1 million came from labor and 2.5 million from agrarians. The remainder were Socialist or Farm-Labor votes. Obviously, neither laborers nor farmers turned out for him in the numbers expected. In the Midwest, fewer than one-third of the votes cast went to LaFollette. Only in Wisconsin, his home state, was he first in the balloting, and only there did the electorate endorse a clear alternative to the normalcy program.[10]

Coolidge's victory was ascribed to various factors—Democratic ineptness, rising grain prices in the West, public apathy, Coolidge's own shrewdness, and so on. Some said the victory was personal and did not reflect public endorsement of Coolidge's party. But the election of 1924 *was* a clear reendorsement of the Republican party and revealed a continued public desire for normalcy. In a sense, 1924 was a repetition of the election of 1920. There was, however, an important difference. In 1920 the electorate had no point of reference for normalcy; then normalcy was little more than a word. In 1924 the electorate had such a reference—the Harding policies which Coolidge now pledged to continue. Voter reendorsement therefore did not occur in a vacuum. By 1924 the whole normalcy concept was so thoroughly entrenched that even the shock effect of scandal and of agrarian insurgency could not dislodge it.

Unquestionably, the major campaign factor was, again, the return of business prosperity. Without such prosperity the election results might have been different. In 1920 normalcy had

10. Election statistics are from MacKay, *The Progressive Movement of 1924*, 219–21, 274.

been merely a synonym for prosperity. In 1924 it was the real thing. Prosperity, after all, represented the successful fulfillment of the normalcy policies and endowed them with validity. Prosperity not only justified Republican conservatives in continuing to hold to their economic and social beliefs but even persuaded many of those with more liberal tendencies that whatever had caused this marvelous advance was worth supporting. Some liberals would even convince themselves that the new economic order accompanying the normalcy program actually possessed "progressive" qualities and represented a logical extension of the progressive spirit.

In this regard, the question often asked is: Where did the progressives and the former public support for progressivism go in the 1920s? It is a mystery that remains to be solved. But a few surprising clues emerge from a careful study of the years 1920–24. Some of this support was garnered by Warren Harding in 1920, and, despite appearances in 1922 and the LaFollette campaign in 1924, a sizable portion of it continued for a time to remain with the Republicans. The specifically pro-LaFollette portion quickly disappeared after 1924 in the increasing apathy and disillusionment concerning politics in general. However, the continuing economic success of the normalcy program retained a peculiar fascination for many middle-class progressives. This fascination might have served as a catalyst for a new and long-lasting political coalition. But such a coalition never fully materialized, since the Republicans under Coolidge, by persistently ignoring the significance of other issues, mainly local and often non-political in nature and affecting the cities and industrial areas of the North and East, failed utterly to exploit it. Ironically, therefore, the lure of normalcy proved to be only temporary for these progressive elements, and they used the Republican party on the national level only as an overnight haven on their way to a permanent refuge with Roosevelt in 1932.[11]

11. Much research needs to be done on the connection between prosperity and progressivism in the maintenance of Republican supremacy during the 1920s. So far, only hints and suggestions have appeared in scholarly writings.

If Coolidge's election assured the continuation of the normalcy program, it nonetheless marked the end of the Harding period. Following the 1924 election, American national politics carried Coolidge's special stamp, as he no longer lived so directly under the shadow of his predecessor. As the New York *Sun* put it: "He has been President by accident. Now he is President in his own right." [12] Unlike Harding, Coolidge was a true conservative and a business fundamentalist in his view of the economic and social order. Where Harding strove for balance in the economic realm, Coolidge made little effort to do so. It was quickly obvious that agrarian interests and other minority groups had been much better able to make their views felt under Harding than under his successor. Indeed, never again during the 1920s would these elements receive so sympathetic a hearing. After 1925, Coolidge rapidly packed regulatory boards and agencies with men who uniformly showed a business bias, causing the *Wall Street Journal* to exult: "Never before, here or anywhere else, has a government been so completely fused with business." [13] Shortly after Harding's death, William McAdoo prophesied that Coolidge would be a more useful instrument of big business than Harding ever was, and this was certainly true.[14] Wall Street consistently found Coolidge to be "sound from every angle," especially after 1925, when Mellon emerged as the most important presidential adviser.[15]

This latter development signified another important change in the operation of government under Coolidge in the years after 1925. Coolidge made no pretense of continuing Harding's "best minds" executive system, even though for a time he retained most of its personnel. He did not consult widely with his cabinet officers, nor did he encourage them to offer him advice. Coolidge viewed anyone as sharp and ambitious as Hoover with extreme suspicion, and referred to him derogatorily as "that Wonder boy." Cabinet replacements (Wallace, who died

12. "Calvin Coolidge As the Victory-Maker," *Literary Digest,* LXXXIII (November 15, 1924), 8, quoting the *Sun.*
13. Arthur M. Schlesinger, Jr., *The Crisis of the Old Order, 1919–1933* (Sentry edition, Boston, 1957), 61, quoting the *Wall Street Journal.*
14. Noggle, *Teapot Dome,* 59, quoting McAdoo.
15. *Wall Street Journal,* December 7, 1923, p. 1.

in October 1924, was supplanted by Howard M. Gore; Hughes, who resigned in 1925, was replaced by Frank B. Kellogg) were generally not well known, and the President made no attempt to integrate them into any over-all executive scheme. Except for Mellon, Coolidge did not fraternize with his cabinet members and, unlike Harding, did not find such sterile relationships disturbing.

Coolidge, of course, brought to the executive branch none of the personal charm or magnetism of his predecessor. While Coolidge's coolness was important in reestablishing the dignity of the presidency, it did little to facilitate consensus or compromise politics. Aloof and impersonal, Coolidge possessed few of the humane qualities that had enabled Harding to survive the years 1921–23 and to successfully create the normalcy program. He was, however, ably suited to be the custodian of that program and neatly supplied the purity and rectitude so badly needed when that program was threatened as a result of the scandals. Harding and Coolidge were not alike, but each in his own way was essential to the success and continuation of the normalcy system.

In his concept of the presidency, Coolidge also did not take up where Harding left off. Had Harding lived, there is every indication that he would have attempted to exercise ever greater presidential power, insert himself more influentially into legislative affairs, and function more directly as head of his party. Continued serious executive-congressional battles were in prospect. Harding was clearly prepared not only to block congressional proposals he did not like but to fight aggressively for those he wanted. Coolidge, on the other hand, represented a return to the image of the presidency that Harding had held originally but had been forced to abandon. Coolidge simply refused to be greatly concerned with congressional squabbles and ignored congressional attempts to embarrass the White House. His contact with congressional leaders was infrequent and perfunctory. He wanted to remain free from legislative entanglement, and generally managed to do so. Even his use of the veto was not a sign of executive involvement, as it had been with

Harding, but of disengagement. Like Harding, Coolidge most enjoyed the ceremonial and figurehead aspects of the presidency. Unlike Harding, Coolidge during his tenure kept himself free to indulge his interests in such activities. Ironically, in both the legislative and the ceremonial areas Coolidge was able to be the president Harding would have liked to be.

Perhaps the molding power of the presidential office and its customary political imperatives might have influenced Coolidge more, as they certainly did Harding, if circumstances had been different. Coolidge, after all, never had to fight for a political program—he was handed one ready-made. He ran on a stand-pat platform, which enabled him to remain politically passive. Unlike the legacy left to Harding by his predecessor, Coolidge's legacy contained mainly solved rather than unsolved problems. The most obvious areas of congressional-executive conflict (e.g., foreign affairs) had already been defused, and as long as no new departures were contemplated or old wounds reopened (e.g., ship subsidies), relative tranquillity could be expected. In short, Coolidge had options that Harding never had —he never *had* to act as an innovator or initiator.

Further, if Democratic opposition had continued as strong as it was in the first session of the 68th Congress, or if the insurgent movement had grown to significant proportions, Coolidge might have been forced to act differently. But after mid-1924, no longer did the halls of Congress ring with so much acrimony and strife. The passing of the investigation mania in the spring of 1924 left most legislators limp and longing for a respite. Meanwhile, Coolidge's obvious purity removed a potential reason for continuing the debate. Indeed, it was impossible for congressmen to outdistance Coolidge in moral rectitude, and many of them made a serious mistake in 1924 in attempting to make the question of presidential morality a political issue.

Significantly, the voters in 1924 gave Coolidge not only a term in his own right but also a "Coolidge congress." The 69th Congress, much to the relief of the White House, was clearly controlled by pro-administration Republicans. Missing were numerous opposition catalysts, among them LaFollette, who died in June 1925. But even before this Congress convened, the trend away from contention was apparent. A subdued and dispirited Democratic and insurgent coalition returned to the Capitol for the second session of the 68th Congress in December 1924. There was no business before that session except for the annual appropriation bills, and Coolidge did nothing to precipitate trouble. His uninspired message was not even delivered in person but read in a monotone by clerks. Even the southern Democratic bloc appeared listless. The election returns, coupled with prosperity, and quickly done their work.

This is not to say that Congress thereafter lapsed into complete inactivity. Many congressmen continued to keep a wary eye on the White House, and dissident farm elements continued to disrupt Republican party harmony by joining with the Democratic minority to attack the administration on such matters as public power and farm policy. But during the remainder of the decade the executive-congressional struggle never approached the heights of 1921–24. Coolidge's desire for disengagement from congressional battles was matched by a congressional reluctance to take new initiatives. For instance, neither Coolidge nor Congress paid the least attention to Harding's western speeches or used them as the basis for any new departures.[16] Except for the few fitful altercations caused by the farm bloc and such urban mavericks as LaGuardia, a general truce settled over American politics. Internal problems in the Democratic party kept it occupied as well as impotent, while most Republicans were content for the moment to savor their party's apparent success. The lack of a dynamic opposition, the absence of an alternative program, continued poor congressional leadership, the soothing effect of prosperity, and a nonaggressive president combined to assuage the desire for change and relegated politics to only secondary importance.

16. Interestingly enough, the major innovations undertaken during these years, some of which grew out of Harding's western speeches (e.g., the successful negotiation of joint federal-state agreements on the use of water sites, etc.), occurred within the executive bureaucracy, especially as the result of activities by Hoover's Commerce Department.

Thus, the Coolidge era of relative tranquillity emerged from the political turbulence and immorality associated with the Harding period. Contrary to Harding's hopes, that period, spanning the years 1920–24, had been marked by anything but reasonableness and an absence of excess. For Harding, normalcy in practice had been far different from normalcy in theory. As president he had had to fight for his basic program and then fight to protect and expand it. He had never had the united support of his party or of its congressional leadership. Moreover, presidential politics had always required more of him than mere attention to formalities or an occasional compromise. Indeed, the years from 1920 to 1924 had been stained by more political greed, frustrated ambitions, warped motivations, and ignoble aspirations than any period since Reconstruction. Insurgency and regional and economic partisanship had threatened at times to make the development of any kind of coherent program virtually impossible. Concomitantly, congressional chauvinism continually endangered the integrity of the presidential office, while the President was forced by changing circumstances to alter drastically not only his tactics but many of his administrative concepts.

Despite these difficulties, and despite the infamous scandals, the years 1920–24 also witnessed the successful creation of the program known as normalcy. That program's short-term achievements were impressive enough—the peace treaties, the Washington Disarmament Conference, reform farm legislation, economy in government, the Budget Bureau, a new tariff, immigration restriction, and a reduction in the national debt and in taxes. But its long-term impact was even more significant. The concept of normalcy set the philosophical and structural framework for the politics and even for the day-to-day operation of the federal government for the remainder of the decade. The belief that there was a "normal way" for politics to function and that the government could be conducted "without excess" undergirded all subsequent attempts in the 1920s to achieve the good life for the American people without unduly compromising with the emerging demands of an urban and highly complicated industrial society. More important, the normalcy program served to bring the nation out of the scare-ridden postwar depression days of Wilson into the buoyant, prosperous years of the middle and late 1920s. Such a result was precisely what normalcy had envisioned in theory and what its chief expounder, Warren Harding, had promised. Ironically, however, although prosperity, government "without excess," a cessation in the executive-congressional struggle, and a figurehead presidency were all part of Harding's aspirations, they were never a part of his life. Only under Coolidge did the theory finally become practice.

A Bibliographical Review

MATERIALS relating to the 1920s are already extensive and are multiplying rapidly. Significant manuscript collections now include: the Warren G. Harding Papers in the Ohio Historical Society Library, Columbus, Ohio; the Herbert C. Hoover Papers in the Hoover Presidential Library, West Branch, Iowa; the Franklin D. Roosevelt Papers in the Roosevelt Library, Hyde Park, New York; the Alfred E. Smith Papers in the New York State Library, Albany, New York; the John W. Davis Papers in the Sterling Memorial Library, New Haven, Connecticut; the Will H. Hays Papers in the Indiana State Historical Society Library, Indianapolis, Indiana; the Henry Cabot Lodge Papers in the Massachusetts Historical Society Library, Boston, Massachusetts; and the Calvin Coolidge Papers, Charles E. Hughes Papers, Thomas J. Walsh Papers, William G. McAdoo Papers, Robert M. LaFollette Papers, George W. Norris Papers, William H. Taft Papers, and William E. Borah Papers, all in the Library of Congress.

Of secondary importance for the decade as a whole, but useful for the early years of the period are: the Joseph S. Frelinghuysen Papers in the Rutgers University Library, New Brunswick, New Jersey; the Albert B. Fall Papers in the University of New Mexico Library, Albuquerque, New Mexico; the Edwin Denby Papers in the Detroit Public Library, Detroit, Michigan; and the James J. Davis Papers in the Library of Congress. Minor collections, which are extremely valuable on the Harding years, are the papers of Walter F. Brown, Cyril Clemens, Harry M. Daugherty, Alfred W. Donithen, Newton D. Fairbanks, Arthur L. Garford, Charles E. Hard, Ray Baker Harris, Malcolm Jennings, Mary E. Lee, E. Mont Reily, F. E. Scobey, and Frank B. Willis, all in the Ohio Historical Society Library.

Indispensable for any evaluation of the early 1920s are the many public documents and government publications that exist. Of course, the *Congressional Record* is most important. In addition, there are numerous congressional hearings and investigations. Most valuable are the Senate hearings on campaign expenses in 1920, the 1922 House investigation of Attorney General Daugherty, the 1923 Senate investigation of the Veterans' Bureau, the 1924 Senate investigation of the oil leases, the 1924 Senate investigation of the Justice Department, and the 1928 investigation of the final disposition of the oil "bribe money." Also significant are the hearings relating to the Emergency Tariff and the Fordney-McCumber tariff, immigration, the ship-subsidy plan, and Mellon's proposed tax legislation. Valuable, too, are the annual reports of the various agencies and departments of government, such as the Interstate Commerce Commission, the Federal Reserve Board, and the departments of the Treasury, Agriculture, Commerce, Labor, the Interior, and the Post Office.

Especially useful are the memoirs, writings, and autobiographies of observers and participants in the Harding-Coolidge era. Among the journalists are Clinton Gilbert, *The Mirrors of Washington* (New York, 1921), and *Behind the Mirrors: The Psychology of Distintegration at Washington* (New York, 1922); Edward G. Lowry, *Washington Close-Ups: Intimate Views of Some Public Figures* (Boston, 1921); Charles Michelson, *The Ghost Talks* (New York, 1944); Thomas L. Stokes, *Chip Off My Shoulder* (Princeton, 1940); and William A. White, *The Autobiography of William Allen White* (New York, 1946). Among the significant writings of political leaders are James M. Cox, *Journey Through My Years* (New York, 1946); William G. McAdoo, *Crowded Years: The Reminiscences of William G. McAdoo* (Boston, 1931); George W. Norris, *Fighting Liberal: The Autobiography of George W. Norris* (New York, 1961); Oscar W. Underwood, *Drifting Sands of Party Politics* (New York, 1931); James E. Watson, *As I Knew Them* (New York, 1936); Calvin Coolidge, *The Autobiography of Calvin Coolidge* (New York, 1929); Andrew W. Mellon, *Taxation: The People's Business* (New York, 1924); Charles Evans Hughes, *The Pathway of Peace* (New York, 1925); James J. Davis, *The Iron Puddler: My Life in the Rolling Mills and What Came of It* (Indianapolis, 1922); Harry M. Daugherty (in collaboration with Thomas Dixon), *The Inside Story of the Harding Tragedy* (New

York, 1932); and Herbert Hoover, *The Memoirs of Herbert Hoover: The Cabinet and the Presidency, 1920–1933* (New York, 1952). Others writings of some value are Irwin H. ("Ike") Hoover, *Forty-Two Years in the White House* (Boston, 1934); Alice Roosevelt Longworth, *Crowded Hours* (New York, 1933); and Edmund W. Starling, *Starling of the White House* (New York, 1946).

Recent scholarship on the 1920s has resulted in myriad articles appearing in scholarly journals, such as the *American Economic Review, American Historical Review, Historian, Journal of Modern History, Journal of Political Economy, American Political Science Review, Political Science Quarterly, Journal of American History, Journal of Negro History, Mississippi Valley Historical Review, Pacific Historical Review, Ohio History,* and *Science and Society.* Far too numerous to list here, a brief representation must include: Wesley M. Bagby, "The 'Smoke Filled Room' and the Nomination of Warren G. Harding," *MVHR,* XLI, No. 4 (March 1955), 657–74; J. Leonard Bates, "The Teapot Dome Scandal and the Election of 1924," *AHR,* LX, No. 2 (January 1955), 303–22; Roy G. Blakey, "The Revenue Act of 1921," *American Economic Review,* XII, No. 1 (March 1922), 75–108; Paul W. Glad, "Progressives and the Business Culture of the 1920's," *JAH,* LIII, No. 1 (June 1966), 75–89; John D. Hicks, "Research Opportunities in the 1920's," *Historian,* XXV, No. 1 (November 1962), 1–13; Arthur S. Link, "What Happened to the Progressive Movement in the 1920's?," *AHR,* LXIV, No. 4 (July 1959), 833–51; Fritz M. Marx, "The Bureau of the Budget: Its Evolution and Present Role," *American Political Science Review,* XXXIX, No. 4 (August 1945), 653–84; Henry F. May, "Shifting Perspectives on the 1920's," *MVHR,* XLIII, No. 3 (December 1956), 405–27; Burl Noggle, "The Twenties: A New Historiographical Frontier," *JAH,* LIII, No. 2 (September 1966), 299–314; Richard B. Sherman, "The Harding Administration and the Negro: An Opportunity Lost," *Journal of Negro History,* XLIX, No. 3 (July 1964), 151–68; James H. Shideler, "The Distintegration of the Progressive Party Movement of 1924," *Historian,* XIII, No. 2 (spring 1951), 189–201; Elmus R. Wicker, "Federal Reserve Monetary Policy, 1922–33: A Reinterpretation," *Journal of Political Economy,* LXXIII, No. 4 (August 1965), 325–43; Robert K. Murray, "President Harding and His Cabinet," *Ohio History,* LXXV, Nos. 2–3 (spring-summer 1966), 108–25; and William A. Williams, "The Legend of Isolationism in the 1920's," *Science and Society,* XVIII (1954), 1–20.

Biographies are plentiful, but some serious gaps exist. There are, for example, no biographies of John W. Davis, Fall, Hays, Daugherty, or Weeks, nor is there yet an adequate treatment of Mellon or, for that matter, of LaFollette and Hoover. Harding biographies range from badly distorted to adequate. Among the former is the recent *The Shadow of Blooming Grove: Warren G. Harding in His Times* (New York, 1968), by Francis Russell. The best-known but also flawed biography is that of Samuel Hopkins Adams, *Incredible Era: The Life and Times of Warren Gamaliel Harding* (Boston, 1939); also well known but defective is the Harding portrait drawn by William Allen White in his *Masks in a Pageant* (New York, 1928). Too superficial but still provocative is Andrew Sinclair's *The Available Man: The Life Behind the Masks of Warren Gamaliel Harding* (New York, 1965). Best on the pre-presidential years is Randolph C. Downes' *The Rise of Warren Gamaliel Harding, 1865–1920* (Columbus, 1970). My own *The Harding Era: Warren G. Harding and His Administration* (Minneapolis, 1969) attempts to give the most complete coverage of the presidential period. Helpful biographies on various members of the Harding-Coolidge official family are Bascom N. Timmons, *Portrait of an American: Charles G. Dawes* (New York, 1953); Russell Lord, *The Wallaces of Iowa* (Boston, 1947); Harvey O'Connor, *Mellon's Millions: The Biography of a Fortune* (New York, 1933); Merlo J. Pusey, *Charles Evans Hughes,* 2 vols. (New York, 1951); Eugene Lyons, *Herbert Hoover: A Biography* (New York, 1964); and the two standard biographies of Coolidge —William Allen White, *A Puritan in Babylon* (New York, 1938), and Claude M. Fuess, *Calvin Coolidge: The Man from Vermont* (Boston, 1940). Better than these last two is the most recent biography of Coolidge: Donald R. McCoy, *Calvin Coolidge: The Quiet President* (New York, 1967).

Other important biographies of varying readability and accuracy are Henry F. Pringle, *The Life and Times of William Howard Taft: A Biography,* 2 vols. (New York, 1939); Homer Socolofsky, *Arthur Capper: Publisher, Politician, and Philanthropist* (Lawrence, Kansas, 1962); Hermann Hagedorn, *Leonard Wood: A Biography,* 2 vols. (New York, 1931); John A. Garraty, *Henry Cabot Lodge: A Biography* (New York, 1953); John

Gunther, *Taken at the Flood: The Story of Albert D. Lasker* (New York, 1960); William T. Hutchinson, *Lowden of Illinois: The Life of Frank O. Lowden,* 2 vols. (Chicago, 1957); Fola and Belle C. LaFollette, *Robert M. LaFollette,* 2 vols. (New York, 1953); Claudius O. Johnson, *Borah of Idaho* (New York, 1936); and Josephine O'Keane, *Thomas J. Walsh: A Senator from Montana* (Francestown, New Hampshire, 1955). Both the Johnson and the O'Keane works should be used with considerable caution.

Monographs and special studies on all aspects of life in the early 1920s abound. Only a limited number can be cited here. The best general work on foreign policy is Selig Adler, *The Uncertain Giant, 1921–1941: American Foreign Policy Between the Wars* (New York, 1965). Somewhat biased in interpretation is Betty Glad, *Charles Evans Hughes and the Illusions of Innocence: A Study in American Diplomacy* (Urbana, Illinois, 1966). Best on the relationship between the United States and the Soviet Union is Robert P. Browder, *The Origins of Soviet-American Diplomacy* (Princeton, 1953). The Washington Conference is adequately treated in a number of books: Raymond L. Buell, *The Washington Conference* (New York, 1922); C. Leonard Hoag, *Preface to Preparedness: The Washington Disarmament Conference and Public Opinion* (Washington, D.C., 1941); and John C. Vinson, *The Parchment Peace: The United States Senate and the Washington Conference, 1921–1922* (Athens, Georgia, 1955). Most useful on American oil diplomacy are Ludwell Denny, *We Fight for Oil* (New York, 1928), and John Ise, *The United States Oil Policy* (New Haven, 1926). The two standard works on war debts are Harold G. Moulton and Leo Pasvolsky, *War Debts and World Prosperity* (New York, 1932), and Harold G. Moulton and Leo Pasvolsky, *World War Debt Settlements* (New York, 1926). Although too moralistic, Denna F. Fleming's two books on the World Court and American relations with the League are still the best: *The United States and the World Court* (New York, 1945), and *The United States and World Organization, 1920–1933* (New York, 1933).

Reliable works on demobilization, inflation, postwar depression, prohibition, and social trends in the early 1920s are Benedict Crowell and Robert F. Wilson, *Demobilization: Our Industrial and Military Demobilization after the Armistice, 1918–1920* (New Haven, 1921); James R. Mock and Evangeline Thurber, *Report on Demobilization* (Norman, Oklahoma, 1944); Paul A. Samuelson and Everett E. Hagen, *After the War, 1918–1920: Military and Economic Demobilization of the United States* (n.p., 1943); Wilson F. Payne, *Business Behavior, 1919–1922: An Account of Postwar Inflation and Depression* (Chicago, 1942); President's Research Committee on Social Trends, *Recent Social Trends in the United States*, 2 vols. (New York, 1933); Herbert Asbury, *The Great Illusion: An Informal History of Prohibition* (New York, 1950); Andrew Sinclair, *Prohibition: The Era of Excess* (Boston, 1962); Norman F. Furniss, *The Fundamentalist Controversy, 1918–1931* (New Haven, 1954); Charles Merz, *The Great American Bandwagon* (New York, 1928); and Robert K. Murray, *Red Scare: A Study in National Hysteria, 1919–1920* (Minneapolis, 1955). Excellent on Wilson's final days in the White House is Gene Smith, *When the Cheering Stopped: The Last Years of Woodrow Wilson* (New York, 1964).

Of primary importance on the political events of the early 1920s are Wesley M. Bagby, *The Road to Normalcy: The Presidential Campaign and Election of 1920* (Baltimore, 1962), and Kenneth C. MacKay, *The Progressive Movement of 1924* (New York, 1947). Badly distorted accounts of Teapot Dome are presented by M. R. Werner and John Starr, *Teapot Dome* (New York, 1959), and Marcus E. Ravage, *The Story of Teapot Dome* (New York, 1924). Morris R. Werner's *Privileged Characters* (New York, 1935), an exposé of all the scandals in the Harding administration, must be used with discretion. The most balanced evaluations of Teapot Dome and its background are J. Leonard Bates, *The Origins of Teapot Dome: Progressives, Parties, and Petroleum, 1909–1921* (Urbana, Illinois, 1963), and Burl Noggle, *Teapot Dome: Oil and Politics in the 1920's* (Baton Rouge, 1962).

The most useful studies on American economic policy, the tariff, immigration, and related matters are Frank W. Taussig, *Some Aspects of the Tariff Question: An Examination of the Development of American Industries Under Protection* (Cambridge, Massachusetts, 1934); J. Marshall Gersting, *The Flexible Provisions of the United States' Tariff, 1922–1930* (Philadelphia, 1932); John Higham, *Strangers in the Land: Patterns of American Nativism, 1860–1925* (New Brunswick, New Jersey, 1955); Joseph Brandes, *Herbert Hoover and Economic Diplomacy: Department of Commerce Policy, 1921–1928* (Pittsburgh, 1962); Herbert Feis, *The Diplomacy of the Dollar: First Era, 1919–1932* (Baltimore, 1950);

Roy G. and Gladys C. Blakey, *The Federal Income Tax* (New York, 1940); Harold L. Reed, *Federal Reserve Policy, 1921–1930* (New York, 1930); and Paul M. Zeis, *American Shipping Policy* (Princeton, 1938).

Good material on business attitudes, labor, and the farm problem during the normalcy era can be found in Irving Bernstein, *The Lean Years: A History of the American Worker, 1920–1933* (Cambridge, Massachusetts, 1960); James W. Prothro, *The Dollar Decade: Business Ideas in the 1920's* (Baton Rouge, 1954); R. R. Enfield, *The Agricultural Crisis, 1920–1923* (London, 1924); James H. Shideler, *Farm Crisis, 1919–1923* (Berkeley, 1957); Robert L. Morlan, *Political Prairie Fire: The Nonpartisan League, 1915–1922* (Minneapolis, 1955); and Theodore Saloutos and John D. Hicks, *Agricultural Discontent in the Middle West, 1900–1939* (Madison, Wisconsin, 1951).

Among the many statistical studies available on the early 1920s, the most pertinent are: National Industrial Conference Board, *Wages in the United States, 1914–1930* (New York, 1931); M. Ada Beney, *Wages, Hours, and Unemployment in the United States, 1914–1936* (Report No. 229, NICB, New York, 1936); *Changes in the Cost of Living, July, 1914–July, 1923* (Report No. 63, NICB, New York, 1923); *Wages, Hours, and Employment in American Manufacturing Industries, July, 1914–July, 1923* (Report No. 62, NICB, New York, 1923); *The Cost of Living Among Wage Earners: Anthracite Region of Pennsylvania, February, 1922* (Special Report No. 21, NICB, New York, 1922); *Wages, Hours, and Employment of Railroad Workers* (Report No. 70, NICB, New York, 1924); and *The Unemployment Problem* (Report No. 43, NICB, New York, 1921).

There is a growing list of theses and dissertations that treat of various aspects of the 1920s, and a resurgent interest of students in the decade threatens to increase the output markedly. Among the most significant for the early years are: Harold F. Alderfer, "The Personality and Politics of Warren G. Harding" (Ph.D. dissertation, Syracuse University, 1928); J. Leonard Bates, "Senator Walsh of Montana, 1918–1924: A Liberal Under Pressure" (Ph.D. dissertation, University of North Carolina, 1952); Robert E. Hauser, "Warren G. Harding and the Ohio Presidential Primary of 1920" (M.A. thesis, Pennsylvania State University, 1967); Mary A. Miller, "The Political Attitude of the Negro: 1920–1932" (M.A.

thesis, Pennsylvania State University, 1968); James H. Shideler, "The Neo-Progressives: Reform Politics in the United States, 1920–1925" (Ph.D. dissertation, University of California, 1945); and Davis H. Stratton, "Albert B. Fall and the Teapot Dome Affair" (Ph.D. dissertation, University of Colorado, 1955).

No bibliographical review of the historical literature of the 1920s could conclude without mentioning the basic general works that cover the period. Certainly the best-known and most popular is Frederick Lewis Allen's *Only Yesterday: An Informal History of the Nineteen-Twenties* (New York, 1931). A remarkable book in many ways, it is nevertheless faulty on the Harding-Coolidge political situation. Somewhat more personal, yet at the same time more factual, is Mark Sullivan's *Our Times: The United States, 1900–1925,* Vol. VI (New York, 1935). Far more balanced and detailed is Frederic L. Paxson's *Postwar Years: Normalcy, 1918–1923* (Berkeley, 1948). *The Crisis of the Old Order, 1919–1933,* by Arthur M. Schlesinger, Jr. (New York, 1957), is highly readable, but its readability cannot mask the fact that it is somewhat distorted in content and biased in tone. Both Karl Schriftgiesser, *This Was Normalcy: An Account of Party Politics During Twelve Republican Years, 1920–1932,* and George Soule, *Prosperity Decade, from War to Depression: 1917–1929* (New York, 1947) are attempts to pin the entire blame for the 1929 debacle on the Republicans. Schriftgiesser even implies that the Republicans, almost singlehanded, also caused World War II. The two best general works yet written on the decade are William E. Leuchtenburg, *The Perils of Prosperity, 1914–1932* (Chicago, 1958), and John D. Hicks, *Republican Ascendancy, 1921–1933* (New York, 1960). This present essay agrees with neither of them on the beginnings of normalcy. Still, Leuchtenburg is excellent in his over-all interpretation, while Hicks, along with Paxson, provides the best factual coverage that can be found.

Index